HEBREWS BIBLE STUDY

A 40-DAY EXPLORATION OF FAITH, PERSEVERANCE, AND GODLY LIVING

40-DAY BIBLE STUDY SERIES
BOOK 10

PETER DEHAAN

Library of Congress Control Number: 2025921632

Published by Rock Rooster Books, Grand Rapids, Michigan

ISBN:

- 979-8-88809-179-1 (e-book)
- 979-8-88809-180-7 (paperback)
- 979-8-88809-181-4 (hardcover)
- 979-8-88809-182-1 (audiobook)

Credits:

- Developmental editor: Julie Harbison
- Copy editor: Robyn Mulder
- Cover design: Cassidy Wierks
- Author photo: Chelsie Jensen Photography

To Susan Wojcik

Series by Peter DeHaan

40-Day Bible Study Series takes a fresh and practical look into Scripture, book by book.

Bible Character Sketches Series celebrates people in Scripture, from the well-known to the obscure.

Holiday Celebration Devotionals rejoice in the holidays with Jesus.

Visiting Churches Series takes an in-person look at church practices and traditions to inform and inspire today's followers of Jesus.

Be the first to hear about Peter's new books and receive updates at PeterDeHaan.com/updates.

CONTENTS

THE BOOK OF HEBREWS

H ebrews is a tough read for many people. They struggle to comprehend it. So if you strain to make sense of this concise 13-chapter book, you're not alone. In this 40-day devotional Bible study, we'll dig into this book to unveil the powerful truths it contains.

First, a bit of background.

We don't know who wrote Hebrews. Traditionally, many people ascribe it to Paul. Yet scholars say the writing style and structure of Hebrews doesn't match Paul's other letters in the Bible. They conclude he isn't the author.

Other considerations are Apollos or Barnabas. Apollos was an educated man who thoroughly knew the Old Testament Scriptures (Acts 18:24).

Barnabas was a Levite who would have likewise known the Old Testament (Acts 4:36). Though either could have written Hebrews, this is mere conjecture.

Interestingly, except for Hebrews 13:19, 22, and 23, the text doesn't use the pronouns *I* and *my* and instead uses *we* and *our*. This suggests the letter to the Hebrews is a group effort. Perhaps—and this is just speculation—Paul, Apollos, *and* Barnabas worked as a team of writers. Also note that the authors are themselves Hebrew and part of their target audience.

Though it would be interesting to know the book's authors, it's more important to consider the book's audience.

The name *Hebrews* suggests it's for the Hebrew people. But does this mean the Jews (that is, the Hebrews) who have converted to Christianity or the Jews who haven't converted? It could be either. The book of Hebrews clearly ties the old covenant of the law with the new covenant of Jesus, so either group could benefit from the text.

Hebrews, which takes less than an hour to read, could help Jewish non-Christians connect the Old Testament with Jesus, revealing him as the Savior the prophets foretold. Yet Hebrews seems more directed to Jewish Christians, to help keep them focused on their newfound faith in Jesus and his new covenant, when they might be tempted to retreat to the familiar old covenant they grew up with.

If you're not Jewish or familiar with Judaism, don't despair.

The book of Hebrews is a great resource for non-Jewish believers—that is, Gentile Christians. It can help us more fully appreciate how Jesus fulfills the Old Testament law when he comes to earth to die for our sins.

Hebrews is a celebration of our faith today *and* the Old Testament traditions that support it. By better understanding Hebrews, we'll better understand our relationship with Jesus.

Who do you think wrote the book of Hebrews? How might that inform your understanding of this book?

[Discover more about the Hebrew people in Exodus 5:3, 9:13–14, and 10:3.]

DAY 1: JESUS PURIFIES US
HEBREWS 1:1–3

After [Jesus] had provided purification for sins, he sat down at the right hand of the Majesty in heaven. (Hebrews 1:3)

The book of Hebrews does not open like most of the other letters in the Bible. Without giving a greeting, stating its recipients, or identifying the author, it launches directly into teaching. As such, we can expect Hebrews to offer a concise and direct read, with no words wasted. The key to understanding Hebrews is patience. We must slow down and take our time. It's not a text to rush through. It's something to savor.

As we read Hebrews, we'll encounter many references to the Old Testament. Though some of these may seem obscure, they're not something we should skim or skip. They're the point of the book and the foundation for our faith. We'll address each reference in this study.

The writers open by confirming that in the past God spoke to the Jewish people through the prophets. We find their writings in the Old Testament: Isaiah, Jeremiah, Ezekiel, and Daniel. Also included are the shorter prophetic works of Hosea, Joel, Amos, Obadiah, Jonah, Micah, Nahum, Habakkuk, Zephaniah, Haggai, Zechariah, and Malachi. Their ministry spans several centuries and covers most of the people's history as a nation.

But now, as well as two thousand years ago, God speaks to his people through Jesus, his Son—and not the prophets. This is the first of many transitions we'll find recorded in the book of Hebrews. Just as God shifts from the prophets to Jesus, he moves from the old covenant to the new covenant, which we see contrasted between the Old Testament and the New Testament of the Bible.

Jesus is God's sole heir. He is the Creator of all things. He displays the Father's glory and serves as the exact portrayal of his nature. And Jesus supports all things simply through his word. He's so amazing.

But there's more. Jesus purifies us from our sins, from the wrong things we have done and will do. He washes us clean. In doing so, he makes us right with Father God and restores us into a relationship with Papa.

He accomplishes all this by dying on the cross as the ultimate sin sacrifice to end all sacrifices. We'll cover this in depth in the days ahead.

Having accomplished all this, Jesus has now returned to heaven and sits at his Father's right hand. If we follow him, we will one day join him there.

What a glorious day that will be.

Which of these characteristics of Jesus are new to you? Have you received the purification Jesus offers?

[Discover more about purification in 1 John 1:9 and 3:3.]

DAY 2: SUPERIOR TO ANGELS
HEBREWS 1:4–14

[Jesus] became as much superior to the angels as the name he has inherited is superior to theirs. (Hebrews 1:4)

After introducing us to Jesus in the opening to Hebrews, our writers shift their discussion to angels. Their Jewish audience knows all about the prophets, and they've read about angels in Scripture, but they don't know Jesus. To help their readers better understand Jesus, the writers compare him to angels.

First, a quick review of angels in the Old Testament.

In their first appearance in the Bible, an angel encourages Hagar after she runs away (Genesis 16:7–

12) and again later after Abraham sends her away (Genesis 21:17). Angels appear to Abraham and later go to Sodom to rescue Lot and his family (Genesis 19:1–26). As Jacob prepares to meet his estranged brother, Esau, God's angels meet him (Genesis 32:1–2). Later, an angel appears to Moses in the burning bush (Exodus 3:2). And so on. Over one hundred verses in the Old Testament mention angels.

Through all this, the Jewish people recognize angels as powerful messengers from God. In chapter one of Hebrews, we learn seven comparisons between Jesus and angels, with multiple Old Testament references.

1. Jesus is God's Son. Angels are not (Psalm 2:7).
2. God promises King David that one of his descendants—who we know refers to Jesus—will rule forever. God will be his father, and he will be God's son. Angels have no such standing (2 Samuel 7:16 and 1 Chronicles 17:12–14).
3. To confirm the superiority of Jesus over the angels, they—and everyone else—will rightly worship him (Psalm 97:7).

4. Jesus has authority over angels (Psalm 104:4).

5. David prophetically declares that God's representative, Jesus, will rule forever and be above all others, implicitly including angels (Psalm 45:6–7).

6. It is Jesus—and not the angels—who creates both the earth and the heavens above (Psalm 8:6 and Zechariah 12:1). He will rule forever (Psalm 102:25–27).

7. It is Jesus—and not angels—whom God invites to sit on his right hand and subject his enemies to him (Psalm 110:1).

These seven statements, which reference eleven Old Testament passages, corroborate that Jesus is greater than the angels.

The concluding statement in this passage confirms Jesus's authority over the angels. Angels are ministering spirits. Their job is to serve (Psalm 91:11, Psalm 103:20, and Matthew 4:11).

This discussion of angels continues in the second chapter of Hebrews, which we'll cover in the days ahead.

How does this passage better inform our understanding of angels? What does it mean to view angels as ministering spirits to serve us?

[Discover more about ministering people in 1 Samuel 2:18, 1 Chronicles 9:13, and Ezra 2:63.]

DAY 3: PAY CAREFUL ATTENTION
HEBREWS 2:1–4

We must pay the most careful attention, therefore, to what we have heard, so that we do not drift away. (Hebrews 2:1)

Though we may think Hebrews chapter 2 will address a new topic, it doesn't. Instead, it builds on the passage before it in chapter 1 about angels. We get confirmation of this by the appearance of the word *therefore* in Hebrews 2:1. Whenever we encounter *therefore* in the Bible, we know that what precedes it ties in with what we're about to read. We must consider both passages together and not isolate one from the other. It's imperative to keep them connected.

The first chapter of Hebrews puts forth much

effort to contrast Jesus with angels. The inescapable conclusion is that Jesus is superior to angels. *Therefore*—as the text says—we need to keep this truth in mind as we consider the next few verses.

In reading about angels in the Old Testament—the Jewish Scriptures—we see that everything they say happens. Their words are binding. People who don't listen to what the angels say—those who violate angelic proclamations—receive a just punishment for their disobedience.

I've yet to find one place in the Bible where what an angel says doesn't happen. Their words are reliable, and the people can count on what the angels say. Since Jesus is greater than the angels—as the writers of Hebrews just proved—how much more confidence should we place in Jesus's words?

Though this may be an obvious conclusion for us today, it would have been foreign to the Hebrew people. The writers strive to make it clear to them: Jesus's words matter, even more so than those of angels.

These words of Jesus point to salvation through him. We dismiss what he says to our own peril, both for the present and for our eternal future.

Though Jesus's words carry authority—even more so than the angels—we don't only have what he says to rely upon. God also testifies to us about Jesus in three tangible ways. These are by "signs and wonders and various miracles and gifts of the Holy Spirit" (Hebrews 2:4, NLT).

We see these three types of testimonies, which confirm Jesus's words, throughout the book of Acts. Acts is a historical record that chronicles the work of Jesus's followers and the early church. Here's an example of each of these testimonies in the book of Acts: signs and wonders in Acts 5:12; miracles in Acts 19:11; and gifts of the Holy Spirit in Acts 19:6.

These three tangible actions give credence to the power and authority of Jesus. We must hold on to this so we don't drift away from our faith in him.

In what ways do we risk drifting away? What gifts of the Holy Spirit are active in your life?

[Discover more about the gifts of the Holy Spirit— that is, spiritual gifts—in 1 Corinthians 12:8–10, 1 Corinthians 12:27–31, and Romans 12:6–8.]

DAY 4: A LITTLE LOWER THAN THE ANGELS

HEBREWS 2:5–10

We do see Jesus, who was made lower than the angels for a little while, now crowned with glory and honor. (Hebrews 2:9)

Hebrews has established that Jesus is superior to the angels. Now we add a third element to the hierarchy: people. God's order is Jesus, angels, and people.

We may think of ourselves as nothing, as we read from Job and David (Job 7:17 and Psalm 8:4). This is in error. In fact, God created us a little lower than the angels. He put everything under our feet. That is, he gave us authority over his creation

(Psalm 8:5–8). This happened when he made Adam (Genesis 1:28–30).

God's intention in the beginning was for everything to be subject to us. But we don't see this in our present reality today because of Adam and Eve's disobedience in the garden of Eden. When they listen to the serpent and believe his lies, they relinquish some of their God-given authority over to him. But this is not directly to the snake. Instead, it's to Satan who controls it.

When Jesus comes to earth, he, too, becomes a little lower than the angels. In this way, his human side is the same as ours. We'll discover the importance of this in the next two readings.

What matters for now is that Jesus doesn't remain a little lower than the angels forever. It's only for a time.

He comes to earth to die in place of us for the wrong things we did and will do. When Jesus overcomes death by rising from the dead, he completes his mission. He returns to heaven. He sits there now. There he's no longer a little lower than the angels. Instead, he resumes his position over them.

In heaven, he wears a crown of glory and honor. He received this for what he did when he died for us, so that we may live with him. Jesus died for us, tasting death for everyone. He suffered death on our behalf so that we wouldn't have to. In doing so, he brings many of us—his sons and daughters—into glory with him.

Jesus condescended himself to come to earth to suffer and die for us to provide us with salvation. All we need to do is receive this gift he offers us.

What do we think of Jesus being made a little lower than the angels, just like us? What do we think about Jesus bringing salvation to us?

[Discover more about salvation through Jesus in Hebrews 1:14, 5:8–10, and 9:27–28.]

DAY 5: BROTHERS AND SISTERS WITH JESUS

HEBREWS 2:11–18

Both the one who makes people holy and those who are made holy are of the same family. So Jesus is not ashamed to call them brothers and sisters. (Hebrews 2:11)

We ended yesterday's passage with the statement that God is bringing many sons and daughters to glory through Jesus (Hebrews 2:10). We see this connection in a figurative sense because when Jesus comes to earth as a little lower than the angels, he is like us. In this way, he connects with us as brothers and sisters. Since he's the Son of God, this makes us sons and daughters of Father God.

More to the point, the writers of Hebrews tell

us that Jesus—as the one who makes people holy—and we—as the ones made holy—are of the same family. Jesus is proud to call us brothers and sisters. We see this prophetically hinted at in Psalm 22:22–23, implied in Isaiah 8:17, and reinforced in Isaiah 8:18. Today's passage in Hebrews is based on these three verses.

When Jesus comes to earth, made a little lower than the angels, he shares in our humanity—in flesh and in blood. He is like us, and he understands us. He knows our struggles because he struggled too. In this way, he can identify fully with us.

Jesus comes to earth to die as a human sacrifice to pay the penalty for all the wrong things all people have done throughout all time. When he does this, he satisfies the sentence our sins deserve. He dies so that we may live. In doing so he makes us right with Father God and reconciles us with him, restoring us into relationship with our Creator.

In this way, Jesus makes us holy.

The holy one makes his creation holy. Because of this, we need no longer fear death or be a slave to it. The devil loses his grip on us. Jesus wins, and the enemy loses. When we follow Jesus, we're on the winning side. We're part of his family, both now and for eternity.

And as his family, Jesus helps us—not angels. He helps the descendants of Abraham. This applies literally to the Hebrews and figuratively to everyone else.

What does it mean that we're part of God's family? If Jesus calls us brothers and sisters, what do we think about calling him our brother?

[Discover more about being part of God's family in Romans 8:17, 2 Corinthians 11:2, Galatians 4:4–6, and Revelation 19:7.]

BONUS CONTENT: HELP WHEN TEMPTED

Because he himself suffered when he was tempted, he is able to help those who are being tempted. (Hebrews 2:18)

When Jesus comes to earth, he is both God and human. This is a paradox, and we must accept it as one, simultaneously perceiving him as both God and man. But this is good.

While a man here on earth, Jesus faces temptations. Yes, Jesus must deal with temptation, just like us.

One notable instance is when Satan tempts Jesus three times in the desert. In each occurrence Jesus prevails and resists the temptation. He quotes

Scripture to rebuff the devil's words (Matthew 4:1–11 and Luke 4:1–13).

We later see Satan trying to tempt Jesus into aborting his mission to die for us by using Peter's well-intended words. Jesus's rebuke, however, isn't to Peter, who uttered the words, but to the deceiver using what the disciple said to tempt Jesus. Our Savior is direct: "Get behind me, Satan!" (Matthew 16:21–23 and Mark 8:31–33).

A third time of temptation may occur right before his death when Jesus asks Papa to "take this cup from me," but he quickly defers to his Father's will and not what he wants (Matthew 26:39, Mark 14:36, and Luke 22:42).

Regarding temptation, the key difference between Jesus and us is that he always resisted the temptations he faced, whereas we aren't always successful.

Jesus experienced temptation in every way, just like us. Yet he never gave in to it. He never sinned. Because of this, we can come to God in confidence that he will help us when temptation confronts us (Hebrews 4:15–16).

What comfort do we have in knowing that Jesus faced temptations when he was here on earth? How can Jesus help us when we face temptation?

[Discover more about temptation, trials, and testing in 1 Corinthians 10:13, 1 Thessalonians 3:2–5, and James 1:2–5.]

DAY 6: FIX OUR THOUGHTS ON JESUS
HEBREWS 3:1–6

Therefore, holy brothers and sisters, who share in the heavenly calling, fix your thoughts on Jesus. (Hebrews 3:1)

In "Pay Careful Attention" (Day 3), we talked about the use of the word *therefore*. Its placement connects what precedes it with what follows it. Today's passage opens with another *therefore*, reminding us that Hebrews 3:1 builds on the previous verse in Hebrews 2:18.

Hebrews 2 ends with a reminder that because Jesus suffered when he was tempted, he knows what it's like and can help us when we're tempted. That's the context for today's verse.

Based on this truth, we should fix our thoughts

on Jesus. This applies to all who "share in the heavenly calling," that is, all who follow Jesus and believe in him—all who acknowledge him as our high priest—which we'll cover on Day 11.

Though Jesus may not be physically with us right now, his experience when he was on earth equips him to know exactly what we're going through. This is so comforting. Jesus—our high priest—understands what we're dealing with.

The writers of Hebrews now contrast Jesus, whom God appointed as our high priest, with Moses, whom God also appointed. Having already contrasted Jesus with the angels, we now distinguish Jesus from Moses.

The Hebrew people are very familiar with Moses, but they don't know Jesus. The books of Exodus, Leviticus, Numbers, and Deuteronomy all center on Moses, portraying him as the Almighty's faithful servant to God's house, that is, the Hebrew people. As a result, the Jews revere Moses and hold him in high esteem.

Yet Jesus is worthy of greater honor than Moses. He is the builder of the house—the Creator—whereas Moses is merely the caretaker of the house. The Creator, Jesus, stands above the created, Moses.

To further confirm that Jesus is more important than Moses, Moses prophesied about Jesus; he bore witness to what was to come (Deuteronomy 18:15–22).

Just as Moses was faithful in God's house long ago, Jesus is faithful over God's house today. And we are God's house (1 Peter 2:4–5).

What are some ways we can keep our thoughts focused on Jesus? How should we react to the truth that we are part of God's house?

[Discover more about us being God's house in 1 Corinthians 3:9.]

DAY 7: HARD HEARTS
HEBREWS 3:7–12

See to it, brothers and sisters, that none of you has a sinful,
unbelieving heart that turns away from the living God.
(Hebrews 3:12)

As the word *therefore* reminds us to connect what follows it with what precedes it, the word *so* serves the same purpose. Today's passage opens with the word *so*. What precedes it in Hebrews 3:6 is the encouragement to cling to our confidence and hope in Jesus.

What follows it, as directed by the Holy Spirit, is a lengthy quote of a passage from Psalm 95:7–11. In it, the psalmist refers to a forty-year period. It's when the Israelites—the Hebrew people—spend four decades in the desert. They have left Egypt behind, but they're yet to enter the land God promised to give them.

It's a journey that should take a couple of weeks, not forty years. It's not that they get lost or forget where they're going, it's that they rebel against God. They don't do this one time, but repeatedly. It is, however, a specific incident that causes God to make them wait forty years. In those forty years, all those who rebelled against him will die. It's their children and grandchildren who will get to enter the promised land.

This rebellion—their chief one—occurs after twelve spies scope out the land God pledged to give them. The dozen spies come back, all giving glowing reports about how wonderful the land is.

Yet ten—the majority—are afraid of the people who live there. These men lack confidence in God and cower in fear over the forces that loom before them. Caleb, implicitly supported by Joshua, urges the people to attack and take the land. They have God's perspective, but they're also in the minority.

It's the opinion of the ten naysayers—the men who lack faith that God will prevail—that the people listen to. The throng weeps. They grumble against Moses and Aaron. They complain, wishing they had died in Egypt instead of in the desert. The ten spies are struck down and killed by a plague (Numbers 13:26–14:38).

God gives them a forty-year sentence in the desert. These people will die there, just as they feared. It's their descendants who will go forward and receive what God wanted to give their parents (Numbers 14:33 and Deuteronomy 1:34–35).

Interestingly, the passage in Psalm 95 refers to a different rebellion, the one at Meribah and Massah (verse 8). The people have no water and complain, demanding Moses give them something to drink. Through God's power, Moses does just that. He strikes a rock and water flows forth (Exodus 17:1–7). Yet this isn't the rebellion that results in the forty-year delay. The Hebrew people also rebel at many other times during their four decades in the desert.

These are all examples of them hardening their hearts against God. This warning to not harden their hearts is a recurring theme in Hebrews. It appears three times, providing emphasis to the rebuke (Hebrews 3:8, 3:15, and 4:7).

The conclusion for the Hebrew people two thousand years ago—as well as for us today—is to not harden our hearts and turn from the living God.

How have we rebelled against God? In what ways might we have hardened our hearts against him today?

[Discover what happens *after* the people harden their hearts and rebel against God, earning them a 40-year time-out in the desert: they rebel again in Numbers 14:39–45.]

DAY 8: ENCOURAGE ONE ANOTHER
HEBREWS 3:13–19

But encourage one another daily, as long as it is called "Today," so that none of you may be hardened by sin's deceitfulness. (Hebrews 3:13)

Besides the connecting words of *therefore* and *so*, we also have the conjunction *but* (as well as *and*). Conjunctions most often occur in the middle of a sentence, clearly linking what appears before them with what happens after. Though less clear, the same applies with sentences that begin with conjunctions, such as today's passage.

Because this verse opens with the word *but*, it encourages us to consider the verses before it to shed insight and gain a deeper understanding of the words that follow it. There we read a warning to make sure we don't have a sinful, unbelieving heart that turns us from the living God.

This caution gives us pause and can even make us shudder. Yet we need not face this struggle alone. Instead, we are to encourage each other on our faith journey every day. We're to do this as long as it is called Today, with a capital T. This means do it now. Don't delay. Putting it off until tomorrow is unacceptable. Do it Today.

Though the Hebrew people lived in community and understood its importance, many in our society today lack this perspective. We tend to live in isolation, focused on ourselves instead of others. Yet our walk with Jesus toward Papa becomes sweeter, deeper, and more fulfilling when we travel with other like-minded believers.

As we walk with each other, we must encourage one another to stay true to our faith, holding our conviction to the end of our lives. In short, we must encourage others to finish strong.

We first saw it in yesterday's reading, and now the writers of Hebrews remind us a second time to not harden our hearts like in the rebellion. (See Day 7: "Hard Hearts.") Though this warning directly addresses the Hebrew Christians, we'll do well to heed this advice today.

When we finish strong, we'll enter our rest. This idea of entering our rest carries a double meaning.

For the people in Moses's day, they could rest once they occupied the land God had pledged to give them. Though they would need to wait to arrive there and take possession of it, once they did, they could rest at last.

Yet this idea of rest also anticipates an even more important event, an everlasting one. When we finish our work here on earth and join Jesus in heaven, we can rest *in* him, rest *through* him, and rest *with* him. And what a glorious rest that will be.

May we keep our focus on him and not turn away so that we may enter our promised rest.

What can we do to encourage one another? What can we do to rest in Jesus Today?

[Discover another verse about Today, with a capital T, in Hebrews 4:7.]

DAY 9: ENTER YOUR REST
HEBREWS 4:1–5

Now we who have believed enter that rest, just as God has said. (Hebrews 4:3)

I n yesterday's reading we talked about encouraging one another so that we may enter our rest. We learned that *rest* carries a double meaning. Just as the Hebrew people could rest once they occupied the land God had promised for them, we can enter the eternal rest God promises to all who follow Jesus.

Yet this idea of *rest* also carries a third meaning, one most significant to the Hebrew people, and one which many of us have lost sight of today.

Through Moses, God told his people to rest on

the seventh day and to keep it holy. Note that God never told them to go to the temple every Sabbath. They were to rest and keep the day holy. The penalty for failing to do so was death (Exodus 35:2). We can ponder if this refers to a physical death or a spiritual one.

The Hebrew people took this seventh day of rest most seriously, even zealously. This may be because when Moses gave them this rule, they'd been slaves for more than four centuries. Their overlords didn't give them the weekend off. They couldn't even take a Sabbath break. They worked—they slaved—seven days a week. The people did this week after week, month after month, year after year. They never had a day to rest. Death was their only release from their endless labor.

So when God tells them to take a Sabbath rest every seven days, they receive this with gladness, ecstatic for a respite from their toil.

Some people today practice this Old Testament command to rest. Though we need not approach it with the religious fervor that the Hebrew people did, our bodies, our souls, and our spirits can benefit from a regular cycle of rest every seven days.

Other people, however, remind us that Jesus fulfills the Old Testament laws. Therefore, the command to rest on the seventh day no longer applies. They are correct in pointing this out.

Yet the idea of resting on the seventh day precedes Moses and the law. It goes back to creation. After God spends six days making our world, its life, and its place in the cosmos, he rests on the seventh day (Genesis 2:2–3).

If God takes time to rest after working six days, we might want to do the same.

What does rest mean to us today? How closely do we need to adhere to Moses's command to rest on the Sabbath and to follow God's example to take a break after six days of work?

[Discover more about rest in Isaiah 57:2 and Revelation 14:13.]

DAY 10: THE WORD OF GOD
HEBREWS 4:6–13

For the word of God is alive and active. Sharper than any double-edged sword, it penetrates even to dividing soul and spirit, joints and marrow; it judges the thoughts and attitudes of the heart. (Hebrews 4:12)

The book of Hebrews continues talking about rest. After discussing a third consideration for rest—to take a break from our work every seven days—the text reverts to its essential meaning: our rest eternal in the afterlife.

This promise of rest for many Hebrew people remains unrealized. Though they hear the good news of Jesus, they do not follow him—which is a form of disobedience—and therefore they will not enter their rest. This idea of disobedience and not entering the promised rest parallels what the Hebrew people experienced in Moses's time. They disobeyed God and died before they could reach their place of rest.

The writers of Hebrews again implore their audience—the Hebrew people back then, as well as us today—to respond now, to do it Today. For a third time, he reminds them—and us—to not harden their hearts (Psalm 95:7–8). Once again, this alludes to their rebellion against God in the desert, which kept them from receiving their promised rest in the land God had for them.

Though Moses led the Hebrew people up to this promised land, God prohibited him—along with his disobedient followers—from entering it. Moving into the land and occupying it falls to Moses's protégé, Joshua.

Joshua does indeed lead God's people—the Hebrews—into the land God promised them through Abraham. They occupy the land and displace much of the people who live there. They conquer it, as God told them to do.

Now they can rest in the land God pledged to give them.

Yet this isn't *the* rest. Metaphorically, we start

with the Sabbath day's rest God takes after creation and Moses commands the people to observe. This once-every-seven-days break reminds us of another rest—an even better one to come. It's one with eternal consequences. We are to do everything to enter this rest and not perish because of disobedience.

God said we can have this eternal rest. We can count on it because the word of God is active. It's alive. It's sharp, penetrating, and discerning. God sees all and knows all.

This verse about the power and purpose of the word of God inspires and encourages many today. Yet we must consider if this refers to the *written* word of God in the Old Testament or the *spoken* word of God through the Holy Spirit.

Two thousand years ago, the written word of God meant the Hebrew Scriptures. This is the Septuagint, a Greek translation of what we now call the Old Testament of the Bible, along with what we refer to as the Apocrypha. This comprised the written word of God two millennia ago.

And we now apply what Hebrews teaches about the word of God to the text that later followed in what we call the New Testament.

Yet, we might be more correct to understand

the word of God in this Hebrews passage as referring to his *spoken* word through the Holy Spirit.

What should we understand the word of God to mean to us today? What do we think about the word of God referring to his spoken word?

[Discover more about the word of God in 1 Chronicles 17:3, Luke 3:1–2, Luke 11:28, Acts 4:31, Ephesians 6:17, and 1 John 2:14.]

DAY 11: THE GREAT HIGH PRIEST
HEBREWS 4:14–5:10

Therefore, since we have a great high priest who has ascended into heaven, Jesus the Son of God, let us hold firmly to the faith we profess. (Hebrews 4:14)

Once again, today's passage opens with the delightful word *therefore*. What precedes it is the command to not harden our hearts and the encouragement to make every effort to enter the rest our all-knowing God promises to give. As a result, we should hold our faith tight and encourage others to do so too.

This verse also mentions the phrase *high priest*, which is absent in the text immediately preceding it.

But the high priest does connect with rest. Here's how.

The book of Hebrews often mentions *high priest*. In fact, this phrase appears more in Hebrews than any other book in the Bible. We've already encountered it in Hebrews 2:17 and Hebrews 3:1. After today's verse, Hebrews mentions *high priest* in fifteen more verses.

This book's teaching about the high priest means much to that day's Hebrew audience. It harkens to the law of Moses and aligns with some of their most meaningful religious rites. Just as the people know much about angels and Moses, they're even more familiar with high priests. The book of Hebrews contrasts each of these three phrases to Jesus to help the Hebrew Christians better understand who he is.

In the Old Testament, Moses's brother Aaron becomes the first priest, the high priest, if you will (Exodus 28:3–4). The priesthood passes from Aaron to his sons, who follow him in service to God. All future priests descend from Aaron, with the high priesthood passing from father to son (Leviticus 16:32).

The Old Testament uses the phrases *high priest* and *chief priest* interchangeably, implicitly with only one high priest serving at a time. When we get to the New Testament, there is still one high priest, but there are multiple chief priests.

The role of the high priest is to serve as a liaison between God and the people. One of the high priest's roles is to offer sin sacrifices to God (Leviticus 9:7). But before he can do this for the people's sins, he must first address his own short-comings (Leviticus 16:6).

The high priest had to offer this sacrifice to atone for the people's sins over and over, year after year. Its coverage didn't last and had to be repeated.

Now Jesus comes as the ultimate high priest, but he's not from the tribe of Levi, a descendant of Aaron, as prescribed by Moses. To show he's a new type of high priest, he comes from the tribe of Judah.

Unlike the high priests in Aaron's line who must cover their own sins before they can address the people's, Jesus has no sin of his own to atone for. He can directly offer a sacrifice for the people's sins. But he doesn't sacrifice an animal as the Old Testament dictates. Instead, Jesus sacrifices himself. In this way he serves as the ultimate sin sacrifice to end all sin sacrifices.

What a relief this must be for the Hebrew

people once they realize that Jesus, as their high priest, takes care of the issue of sin with finality. Through him, they—and we—permanently enter our rest.

Jesus doesn't merely assume this role of high priest. Father God assigns it to him (Psalm 110:4, as seen in Genesis 14:18).

Jesus becomes our high priest in the order of Melchizedek. We'll cover him in Day 16. Until then, know that Melchizedek is a mysterious man who points to Jesus.

What does it mean to us that Jesus is our high priest? Do our actions and attitudes show that we believe Jesus has permanently covered our sins?

[Discover more about Melchizedek in Genesis 14:17–24.]

BONUS CONTENT: HEBREWS IN THE OLD TESTAMENT

But God said to him, "You are my Son; today I have become your Father." (Hebrews 5:5, which quotes Psalm 2:7)

The book of Hebrews has forty-two places —in thirty-nine verses—that reference Old Testament passages. Given that the purpose of the letter to the Hebrew Christians is to help them connect their faith in Jesus with the Old Testament Scriptures, we'd expect to see many references. Yet Hebrews doesn't have the most. Both Matthew and Romans have more, at fifty and fifty-eight verses, respectively.

Here are the forty-two places where Hebrews connects with Old Testament passages, with Psalms leading all others with eighteen references, followed by Deuteronomy with six, and Genesis with four:

- Hebrews 1:5 quotes Psalm 2:7
- Hebrews 1:5 also quotes 2 Samuel 7:14 and 1 Chronicles 17:13
- Hebrews 1:6 alludes to Deuteronomy 32:43
- Hebrews 1:7 quotes Psalm 104:4
- Hebrews 1:9 references Psalm 45:6–7
- Hebrews 1:12 comes from Psalm 102:25–27
- Hebrews 1:13 quotes Psalm 110:1
- Hebrews 2:6–8 quotes Psalm 8:4–6
- Hebrews 2:12 quotes Psalm 22:22
- Hebrews 2:13 quotes Isaiah 8:17
- Hebrews 2:13 also quotes Isaiah 8:18
- Hebrews 3:5 cites Numbers 12:7
- Hebrews 3:7–11 quotes Psalm 95:7–11
- Hebrews 3:15 quotes Psalm 95:7–8
- Hebrews 4:3 and 5 both quote Psalm 95:11
- Hebrews 4:4 references Genesis 2:2
- Hebrews 4:7 again quotes Psalm 95:7–8
- Hebrews 5:5 quotes Psalm 2:7
- Hebrews 5:6 quotes Psalm 110:4

- Hebrews 6:14 alludes to Genesis 22:17
- Hebrews 7:17 again quotes Psalm 110:4
- Hebrews 7:21 quotes more of Psalm 110:4
- Hebrews 8:5 references Exodus 25:40
- Hebrews 8:7–12 quotes Jeremiah 31:31–34
- Hebrews 9:20 quotes Exodus 24:8
- Hebrews 10:5–7 quotes Psalm 40:6–8
- Hebrews 10:16 quotes Jeremiah 31:33
- Hebrews 10:17 quotes Jeremiah 31:34
- Hebrews 10:30 quotes Deuteronomy 32:35
- Hebrews 10:30 also quotes Deuteronomy 32:36 and Psalm 135:14
- Hebrews 10:37 quotes Isaiah 26:20 and Habakkuk 2:3
- Hebrews 10:38 quotes Habakkuk 2:4
- Hebrews 11:5 references Genesis 5:24
- Hebrews 11:18 quotes Genesis 21:12
- Hebrews 12:5–6 quotes Proverbs 3:11–12
- Hebrews 12:13 quotes Proverbs 4:26
- Hebrews 12:18–20 references Exodus 19:12–13

- Hebrews 12:21 alludes to Deuteronomy 9:19
- Hebrews 12:26 quotes Haggai 2:6
- Hebrews 12:29 quotes Deuteronomy 4:24
- Hebrews 13:5 quotes Deuteronomy 31:6
- Hebrews 13:6 quotes Psalm 118:6–7

What do you think about Jesus being God's son? What do you think about your parents and your biological or spiritual children?

[Discover more about fathers and sons in Proverbs 1:8, Malachi 3:17, Luke 2:48, and 2 Timothy 1:2.]

DAY 12: TIME TO TEACH
HEBREWS 5:11–14

In fact, though by this time you ought to be teachers, you need someone to teach you the elementary truths of God's word all over again. You need milk, not solid food! (Hebrews 5:12)

The authors of Hebrews write that they have much more to say about this topic, that is, referring to Jesus as the high priest and the allusion to Melchizedek. But they can't. The people aren't ready to hear what the writers want to say. In fact, they aren't even trying to understand.

It's as if they've given up and don't want to grow in their newfound faith. They're content to coast through their life only knowing the basics and nothing more. They're happy to be spiritual kids and don't want to grow up to be responsible followers of Jesus.

Though the audience—specifically Jewish Christians—should be teachers by this time, they haven't yet mastered the "elementary" truths of God's word. This implies they're still in elementary school and not yet ready to move beyond it.

They crave milk and can't handle solid food.

Just as a baby needs milk and can't yet digest anything else, these followers of Jesus are still babies in their faith, even though they should have grown up by now. They should be eating solid spiritual food and no longer subsisting only on milk.

They are infants in Jesus and don't know about the teaching of righteousness—also known as right living. Just as babies and young children don't know the right way to behave, these followers of Jesus likewise struggle with their behavior.

They're behaving like immature believers and not exhibiting the mature actions that should accompany a more established faith. These baby Christians need to grow up. They need to stop acting like little kids.

We must, however, be careful with this teaching. We don't need to change our behavior to earn our salvation. Instead, after Jesus saves us, we decide to act differently in response to what he has done for us.

Everyone accepts Jesus with the faith of a child (see Matthew 18:2–4), but there's an essential need to advance beyond that. All of us—the Hebrew Christians then and us today—must mature in our faith and move beyond childlike simplicity.

How can we grow in our understanding of Jesus? What should we do differently in response to what Jesus has done for us?

[Discover more about baby Christians in 1 Corinthians 3:1–2.]

DAY 13: ON TO MATURITY
HEBREWS 6:1–3

*Therefore let us move beyond the elementary teachings about
Christ and be taken forward to maturity.* (Hebrews 6:1)

A t this point in our study, the word *therefore*
should jump out at us. We must be ready
to dig into it with expectation. The
preceding passage talks about infant Christians who
can only drink spiritual milk. This means we need
to move beyond the basics—the elementary teachings—and mature in our relationship with Jesus.

As established followers of the Messiah, we
should no longer need to repeat the fundamentals
of our faith. With our foundation already laid, we
need not redo it. We must move beyond the basics.

Yet the writers of Hebrews hold concern for their audience. They're stuck at the foundational level of their faith, and they're content to stay there.

What are these essential truths that they—and we—should know about? Given the passage's context, we need to understand them on a basic level. Let's do that.

First, we must repent—that is, turn away from and go in the opposite direction—of the things we've done wrong, of our sins. Many today view the word *sin* as a mean- spirited, judgmental perspective. But the truth is we all fall short of God's expectations (Romans 3:23). We need a better solution. We need Jesus if we are to receive eternal life (Romans 6:23).

Next, we need to follow Jesus and believe in him through faith. It's by his grace—his goodness that we don't deserve—that we receive our salvation. We can't earn it by following a bunch of rules or striving to do good, so let's stop trying. Instead, we're saved through faith (Ephesians 2:8–9).

The third foundational truth is about "cleansing rights," which most versions of the Bible call baptism. But the reference carries a double meaning, which the Hebrew audience will appreciate.

Baptism is a New Testament word and rite. The Old Testament connection alludes to ceremonial cleansings (Exodus 30:18–21, Leviticus 16:4, and Leviticus 16:23–28).

The fourth basic teaching is about the laying on of hands. This, too, carries a double meaning. This also was part of the Hebrew tradition (Exodus 29:10–19, Leviticus 4:15, and Leviticus 16:21). The New Testament connection is to heal people (Luke 4:40) and, even more so, to impart the Holy Spirit (Acts 8:15–17 and 2 Timothy 1:6).

Fifth is the resurrection of the dead. As followers of Jesus, when our bodies die, we'll rise from the dead and live with him forever (1 Thessalonians 4:16–17).

Finally, the sixth item is eternal judgment. Judgment occurs throughout the Old Testament (Deuteronomy 32:40–41 and Isaiah 3:14). It's something the Hebrew people feared. This idea of judgment carries over into the New Testament for those who don't know and follow Jesus (2 Peter 2:4–10). Yet for those who put their trust in Jesus, eternal judgment is something to anticipate because we will receive a reward (Romans 5:16 and 2 Corinthians 5:10).

Which of these six elementary items do we need to give more attention to? How do we view eternal judgment?

[Discover more about eternal life in John 10:28, 1 Timothy 1:16, and 1 John 5:11.]

DAY 14: FINISH STRONG
HEBREWS 6:4–12

We want each of you to show this same diligence to the very end, so that what you hope for may be fully realized.
(Hebrews 6:11)

Today's reading opens with a troubling passage. It says that for those who fall away from Jesus's saving work, it's impossible for them to be brought back. It would be like crucifying Jesus again. There are multiple ways to interpret what this means and little agreement over it.

Yet we need not worry about this warning if we remain diligent through the rest of our lives and finish strong. Let's focus on that. When we do, we need not concern ourselves about falling away or the impossibility of coming back. It becomes a nonissue.

Consider what we can learn from fields.

The rain falls on them and seeds grow, producing a crop for the farmers. It's a blessing from God. Yet other fields receive the same rain and produce a worthless yield of thorns and thistles. It receives a curse. The only solution is to burn it.

What crop are we growing for Jesus? What are we producing? Is it a bountiful harvest that receives God's blessing? Or is it thorns and thistles that receive the fire of judgment? Note that our crop doesn't earn our salvation. Instead, the harvest we produce is in response to what Jesus did for us by saving us.

As followers of Jesus, we could perceive this warning of fire as a threat, but a better interpretation is to receive it as encouragement. Through our salvation, we can expect good as a result. God is just and will remember our work—what our crops produce—and our love for him as we help and encourage others on their faith journey.

In doing this, we must be diligent to the very end of our lives. We must finish our race strong and not coast to the finish line (1 Corinthians 9:24),

When we do this, we'll fully realize our hope in him, our eternal destiny with Jesus in heaven.

In short, we must not grow lazy. We must not become complacent. Instead, we should imitate the faith and patience of those who've gone before us and inherited the outcome Jesus promised.

Likewise, we can become people others want to imitate. We can guide them on their faith journey and into heaven.

What should we do to finish strong? How can we live lives worthy of imitation?

[Discover more about finishing strong in Luke 14:28–30, Galatians 6:9, Philippians 3:14, and Hebrews 12:1.]

DAY 15: THE INNER SANCTUARY
HEBREWS 6:13–20

We have this hope as an anchor for the soul, firm and secure. It enters the inner sanctuary behind the curtain. (Hebrews 6:19)

Though Hebrews talks a lot about Abraham in the second half of the book, at this point we've only had one brief mention of him (Hebrews 2:16). Hebrews tells us three things about Abraham: his interaction with Melchizedek in chapter 7, his great faith in chapter 11, and God's promise to him here in the latter half of chapter 6.

There are many promises to Abraham which connect and build upon each other in the Old

Testament. The first is that God will make Abraham's name great and bless him to bless others, ultimately through his descendant Jesus (Genesis 12:1–3). Next, God promises Abraham that his offspring will be as numerous as the stars in the sky (Genesis 15:4–5). And later that he will be the father of many nations (Genesis 17:4 and 21:12–13).

After Abraham's son Isaac is born, God tests Abraham's faith by asking him to sacrifice Isaac. When Abraham proves he trusts God above all else, the Almighty spares Isaac and reiterates these promises to the faithful patriarch (Genesis 22:1–18).

The Hebrew people know well the Old Testament principle that to verify something requires at least two witnesses (Deuteronomy 17:6 and 19:15).

With this concept in mind, God makes a promise, *and* he swears to it (Psalm 110:4). This provides a testimony of two witnesses: a promise *and* an oath. Since there is no greater authority for him to swear by, Gods swears by himself, as the ultimate authority. The promise and the oath provide double confirmation to the Hebrew people that God will do what he says.

The direct promise to Abraham is a son, Isaac,

while the secondary promise to the Hebrew people —and to us—is Jesus, Abraham's distant descendant and the Savior of the world.

We place our hope in Jesus. This hope anchors our soul. It allows us to enter the inner sanctuary behind the curtain that only the high priests can enter (Leviticus 16:2–3).

In the Old Testament, God gives Moses specific instructions about the construction of the tabernacle (which Solomon later applies to the temple). A key element of this is the inner sanctuary, the Most Holy Place. There, a heavy curtain blocks access, which symbolically separates the people from God. Only the high priest can enter this area and then only once a year after performing the required rituals and making the prescribed sacrifices (Exodus 26:31–35 and Leviticus 16:15–24).

Yet Jesus becomes a high priest, in the order of Melchizedek. He enters the Most Holy Place on our behalf. When he dies on the cross for us and our sins, this curtain in the temple rips in two, from top to bottom (Matthew 27:51).

In doing so, Jesus allows us to approach God on our own with no priest needed to act as our intermediary.

In what ways do we still rely on others—ministers, clergy, and priests—to connect us to God? How can we realize the direct access to the Almighty that Jesus provides?

[Discover more about the Most Holy Place in the temple that King Solomon builds in 1 Kings 6–8.]

DAY 16: A PRIEST LIKE MELCHIZEDEK

HEBREWS 7:1–10

*Without father or mother, without genealogy, without
beginning of days or end of life, resembling the Son of God,
[Melchizedek] remains a priest forever.* (Hebrews 7:3)

We've briefly mentioned Melchizedek, who's already shown up three times in the book of Hebrews. And we'll see him six more times here in Chapter 7. Interestingly, this character from Genesis only appears twice in the Old Testament. Even so, the Hebrew audience would know all about him.

This mysterious character of Melchizedek interacts with Abraham after the patriarch defeats Lot's captors and liberates his nephew, the rest of the town, and their possessions (Genesis 14:8–17). When Abraham returns victorious, Melchizedek, the king of Salem, meets Abraham and provides him with bread and wine. He blesses Abraham, who gives him a tenth of the plunder (Genesis 14:18–20).

On the surface, this seems like a straightforward story. Yet embedded in it is mystery and wonder. Today's passage in Hebrews explains why.

First, Melchizedek means "king of righteousness." Next comes the confirmation that he's a priest of God Most High. The third element is that Salem—his kingdom—means peace. Interestingly, the city of Salem occurs nowhere else in the Bible except in this passage regarding Melchizedek.

Combining these three facts, we see Melchizedek is a priest and a king of righteousness who rules in peace.

At this point, the book of Hebrews piles onto the mystery. It proclaims that Melchizedek has no father or mother, no genealogy, and lives eternally without beginning or end. As such, he remains a priest forever, a never-ending priesthood.

And there's one more thing. He resembles the Son of God. Though the writers of Hebrews stop short of calling him *the* Son of God or as proclaiming him Jesus, his characteristics parallel Jesus's.

Though Jesus physically has a mother and a father, spiritually he has no genealogy, and he lives eternally with no beginning or end. And, through his death on the cross and resurrection from the dead, he remains a priest forever, in the order of Melchizedek (Psalm 110:4).

The Hebrew people know well the story about Abraham and Melchizedek. They've heard David's Psalm about the coming Savior being a priest forever in the order of Melchizedek. And now they can connect Jesus with this mysterious Old Testament character.

Though Moses institutes the idea of God's people having priests to guide them, it doesn't start with Moses. Melchizedek is the Bible's first mention of a priest. This occurs more than four centuries before Moses. Melchizedek is the forerunner of God's priestly line through Aaron and his descendants. Melchizedek precedes Aaron as God's first priest.

There's also the tithe, a gift of ten percent. Moses also institutes the practice of the tithe, but Scripture's first mention of giving a tenth occurs when Abraham gives it to Melchizedek. Abraham tithes to Melchizedek long before Moses commands it.

Jesus is a priest like Melchizedek, who both precedes and transcends the law of Moses.

How should we view the similarities between Melchizedek and Jesus? How should we react, knowing that both priests and tithes originated four centuries before Moses instituted them?

[Discover more about priests in Romans 15:15–16, 1 Peter 2:4–9, and Revelation 20:6.]

BONUS CONTENT: TEN PERCENT

Abraham gave him a tenth of everything. (Hebrews 7:2)

The Old Testament requires the people to give ten percent to God, a tithe. In fact, there are two annual tithes and a third one every three years. This results in an average of 23.3 percent. That's a lot.

The New Testament, however, never commands us to tithe. Its only mentions of the concept refer to the Old Testament practice. Therefore, since Jesus fulfills the Old Testament, we can disregard the command to tithe today, right? Maybe. Maybe not.

Consider two truths. First, Abraham's gift of ten percent of the spoils to Melchizedek predates

Moses's command to tithe. Second, Melchizedek is an Old Testament representation of Jesus. So perhaps we should tithe today.

This is a worthy consideration, yet we realize that Abraham offers his gift freely and chooses the amount.

With us giving to Jesus, may we follow Abraham's example and not feel bound by Moses's command. It's a gift we present freely and not a rule we must follow.

How should we view the practice of tithing today? How can we best give our resources to Jesus?

[Discover more about tithing—of giving a tenth— in Matthew 23:23, Luke 11:42, and Luke 18:9–14.]

DAY 17: WEAK AND USELESS
NO MORE
HEBREWS 7:11–19

The former regulation is set aside because it was weak and useless (for the law made nothing perfect). (Hebrews 7:18–19)

To help the Hebrew followers of Jesus better understand their new faith, the writers of this letter contrast what was to what is.

First, there is the old priesthood through Aaron and his descendants, with a new priesthood through Jesus, in the order of Melchizedek. Second, only the high priest can go behind the curtain to the Most Holy Place and approach God directly. Now, through Jesus, this curtain that separates us from

God rips open, and we can approach the Father ourselves with no intermediary (Hebrews 6:19–20).

Why did God change his expectations? Why did he do away with the existing covenant with his people to offer them a new one? We'll explore the new covenant in depth in Hebrews 8, but for now, know that the simple reason for a new covenant is because the old one didn't work.

From a human standpoint, when something doesn't work, we shouldn't persist in it. Instead, we should take a fresh approach. That's exactly what God does. The law he gave Moses and the priesthood that surrounded it failed to move his people toward the perfection he desired.

He needed to make a new way through Jesus, who becomes a permanent priest in the order of Melchizedek, not in the order of Aaron.

A change in the priesthood means changing the law that surrounds it.

The first priest, Melchizedek, existed before God revealed his law through Moses. The second priesthood, through Aaron and his descendants, accompanied the Old Testament law and regulations. And the new priesthood, through Jesus, removes the Old Testament requirements to provide a fresh path, making Jesus the only way to approach God (John 14:6).

The former priesthood came through Aaron, from the tribe of Levi. To make sure everyone understands that Jesus's priesthood is different, he comes from the line of Judah. Moses never talks about priests coming from Judah's descendants, only Levi's.

The Hebrew people may have been uncomfortable knowing that Jesus as their priest did not descend from the tribe of Levi. This change, however, sends a clear signal of God instituting something new.

Jesus becomes a priest not based on law or ancestry but on the power of his raised-from-the-dead sacrifice and life eternal in heaven. He is our forever priest, like Melchizedek (Psalm 110:4).

God sets aside what was to bring about something new.

The old way was weak and useless because following a bunch of rules can't make anyone perfect. (Yet without the law, we wouldn't know we need Jesus to save us.) That's why God offers a better way. He offers us hope through Jesus so that we can draw close to Father God.

What does our hope in Jesus look like? In what ways are we continuing to follow a list of rules?

[Discover more about hope in Acts 26:6–7, Romans 5:1–5, 1 Corinthians 13:13, Galatians 5:5, 1 Thessalonians 1:3, and 1 Peter 1:3.]

DAY 18: A PERMANENT PRIESTHOOD
HEBREWS 7:20–28

Unlike the other high priests, [Jesus] does not need to offer sacrifices day after day, first for his own sins, and then for the sins of the people. He sacrificed for their sins once for all when he offered himself. (Hebrews 7:27)

We transition from yesterday's passage to today's with the conjunction *and*. This shows a connection between the two. The change in priesthood we talked about yesterday comes with an oath (see Day 15: "The Inner Sanctuary").

Though other priests assume their roles without an oath, this is not the case with Jesus. God has declared that Jesus will be a priest forever (Psalm

110:4). God does not lie or change his mind (1 Samuel 15:29). Therefore, we can count on what he says.

Because Jesus assumes the priesthood through God's oath, this guarantees us a far better covenant than what the Old Testament law provided.

Many priests lived prior to Jesus. They served and died, and then another priest replaced them. Not so with Jesus. He lives forever. Because he lives on, no one needs to replace him. This means he serves as our permanent priest.

His eternal nature means that he saves us completely, giving us a forever solution to the problem of our sin. This allows us to approach Papa directly through Jesus. As a bonus, Jesus is there in heaven to intercede for us as his followers.

Jesus fully meets our need. Note that the text doesn't say *needs*, plural. The one singular need above all others is to be made right with Father God and brought into his presence. Jesus does that. He is worthy to do that because Jesus is holy, sinless, pure, set apart, and exalted more than anything else in heaven.

These five characteristics differentiate him from all the other high priests who preceded him. While they offered daily sacrifices for their sins and for the people's, Jesus doesn't need to do this.

Jesus sacrifices himself once and for all, for all the sins of everybody, throughout all time. The other priests served in their weaknesses, while Jesus serves forever in strength, having been made perfect.

In this way, Jesus serves as a permanent priesthood for us.

What does it matter to us that Jesus's priesthood comes from an oath by the Father? What does it mean to us that Jesus is our forever priest?

[Discover more about our priesthood through Jesus in 1 Peter 2:4–10.]

DAY 19: A NEW COVENANT
HEBREWS 8:1–6

The ministry Jesus has received is as superior to theirs as the covenant of which he is mediator is superior to the old one.
(Hebrews 8:6)

Hebrews 7 explains about the need for a new priesthood to replace the old one, one which the Hebrew people are most familiar with. Lest there be any doubt, Jesus is this new high priest. But unlike all those high priests who descended from Aaron and preceded him, Jesus as our high priest is unique.

After his resurrection from the dead, Jesus ascends into heaven. He sits at the right hand of the Father's throne. There, Jesus serves in the heavenly sanctuary—the true tabernacle. God himself established this supernatural temple, one far superior to the one built on earth by human hands.

This tabernacle here on earth, along with the temple that replaced it, serves as a mere copy of the original one in heaven, a shadow of what exists in the supernatural realm. Though the heavenly version far exceeds its earthly counterpart, the two parallel each other, with the earthly tabernacle revealing truth to us about the heavenly one.

We get a sense of the importance of their similarity because God warned Moses to build the tabernacle exactly how the Almighty had instructed his servant (Exodus 25:40). This occurred when Moses went up Mount Sinai and spent forty days with God to receive detailed instructions about the tabernacle, worship, and right living (Exodus 24–31).

If it's critical for the construction of the tabernacle on earth to match what's in heaven, there must be a reason for it.

I sense the earthly tabernacle/temple connects with the supernatural one in heaven, linking them together. When Jesus dies and the veil in the temple tears in half here on earth, I envision the corresponding veil in the heavenly counterpart simultaneously rending. On earth this symbolically shows we have direct access to God in the Most Holy Place, whereas in heaven our access is tangible to the very throne of the Father and his presence. This, of course, is merely how I envision it.

Returning to today's text, this discussion about the earthly tabernacle mimicking the superior one in heaven shows that Jesus's ministry is in the same way superior to the priesthood of the Old Testament. It also shows us that the new covenant through Jesus, which he mediates, is likewise superior to the old one.

The new covenant offers us better promises. It pledges to give us forgiveness of sin and life eternal with God in heaven.

In what other ways might it be important for the earthly tabernacle to match the model in heaven? How is Jesus's ministry superior to that of the Old Testament high priests?

[Discover more about the tabernacle in Acts 7:44–50 and Revelation 15:5.]

BONUS CONTENT: OFFER GIFTS AND SACRIFICES

Every high priest is appointed to offer both gifts and sacrifices, and so it was necessary for this one also to have something to offer. (Hebrews 8:3)

I n contrasting the old ways with the new ways —the old covenant with a new covenant— the writers of Hebrews mention offering gifts and sacrifices to God.

We easily see this through all the rituals and rites commanded in the Old Testament for the priests to perform, especially the high priests. Through this they offer both gifts and sacrifices to God.

How does Jesus, as our high priest today, offer gifts and sacrifices?

His death on the cross is a once-and-for-all human sacrifice to replace the need for ongoing animal sacrifices. Through his sacrifice he offers us the gift of salvation. That is, Jesus forgives our sins and restores us into a right relationship with Father God.

Yet Jesus's saving work is not only a gift to us, it's also a gift to Papa. He longs to be in relationship with us, and Jesus makes it happen.

Thank you, Jesus, for offering gifts and sacrifices.

How should we respond to Jesus's gift of salvation? What does it mean that Jesus restores us into a right relationship with Father God?

[Discover more about being restored in Acts 3:17–23 and 1 Peter 5:10.]

DAY 20: THE OLD COVENANT IS OBSOLETE

HEBREWS 8:7–13

By calling this covenant "new," he has made the first one obsolete; and what is obsolete and outdated will soon disappear. (Hebrews 8:13)

Today's passage in Hebrews mostly comprises a long quote from the prophet Jeremiah (Jeremiah 31:31–34). Serving as suitable bookends to this quotation, the writers of Hebrews talk about the old covenant and the new covenant. The old covenant is incomplete, the new covenant makes the former obsolete and outdated, and the old covenant will soon disappear.

Had the old covenant worked, God wouldn't have needed to replace it with a better one. Yet God did. He found fault with the first covenant as being inadequate. But this isn't something he decides when he sends Jesus to earth in the New Testament. This is something he determined long before, which Jeremiah prophesied for us in the Old Testament. This proves God already had a new covenant planned prior to Jesus coming to earth in human form.

About six centuries before Jesus's earthly arrival, the prophet Jeremiah records God's words for us. At that time, God declares that in the future he will make a new covenant with his people, with the people of Israel and of Judah.

This new covenant will not be like the old one Moses gave them after they left Egypt, because the people were unfaithful to that covenant over and over. They strayed from God repeatedly. They turned their backs on him. Because of this, God turned away from them. As punishment, the nation of Israel is conquered and deported. Later, the same thing happens to the nation of Judah.

But the good news, God says to Jeremiah, is that he'll make a new covenant with them. He'll be their God, and they'll be his people. Everyone will know God, regardless of their economic or societal standing. He will forgive all the wrong things they've done and remember their sins no more.

This doesn't mean they won't sin. It means God wipes their record clean and forgets, as if their sins never happened.

If God forgives our sins, there is no reason for us to hold on to them. In fact, it's disrespectful to Jesus when we wallow in guilt over what he has already forgiven and forgotten.

Can we honestly say that he is our God and we are his people? How well do we do at believing God has forgiven and forgotten our sins?

[Discover more about God forgetting our sins in Isaiah 43:25 and Acts 3:19.]

DAY 21: ANNUAL SACRIFICE
HEBREWS 9:1–7

But only the high priest entered the inner room, and that only once a year, and never without blood. (Hebrews 9:7)

Today's passage opens with an overview of God's earthly sanctuary. The Hebrew people would be familiar with these details, so the writers of this letter don't need to explain them. This is not the case with us today. The rooms, their contents, and the ceremonies that took place there are both foreign and mysterious to us.

God's dwelling place on earth was originally the tabernacle and later the temple that replaced it (Exodus 25:8–9). They both contained two rooms or sections. The first was the Holy Place, and the second was the Most Holy Place, which some versions of the Bible call the Holy of Holies. Given that the text says a second curtain separated these two rooms, implicitly a first curtain separated them from the outer courtyard that surrounded them.

The first section was the Holy Place, also referred to as the outer room. It contained a lampstand (Exodus 25:31–40) and a table (Exodus 25:23–30) where the holy bread—the bread of the Presence—sat (Exodus 25:30).

The priests would regularly go into this outer room to perform various ceremonies and carry out their ministry (such as Exodus 28:29–43, Exodus 29:30, Leviticus 6:30, and Leviticus 10:18).

At the back of the Holy Place hung a second curtain, a veil. It blocked access to the Most Holy Place. This area contained the incense altar (Exodus 30:1–10) and the ark of the covenant (Exodus 25:10–22). Both were overlaid with gold.

The ark of the covenant contained three things. First was a jar of manna, which God provided to feed his people while they were in the desert (Exodus 16:31–35 and Deuteronomy 8:3). Next was Aaron's staff that budded, confirming him as God's choice to serve as priest (Numbers 17:1–11). And last were the stone tablets that contained the covenant God gave to Moses (Exodus 31:18 and Exodus 32:15–16) when he spent forty days on Mount Sinai (Exodus 34:28). Above the ark were two cherubim sculptures (Exodus 25:17–22).

This Most Holy Place certainly contained ornate and expensive works, but only a few people ever saw it. Only the high priest could enter this inner room and then just once a year. He did this to offer an annual sacrifice—a sacrifice of blood, much blood—to atone for his sins and the sins of the people.

This is the annual Day of Atonement (Leviticus 16:32–34). It foreshadows what Jesus comes to do when he dies for our sins.

What details about the tabernacle most intrigue you? Why did the high priest have to atone for the people once a year?

[Discover more about the Day of Atonement in Leviticus 16.]

DAY 22: A NEW ORDER
HEBREWS 9:8–10

They are only a matter of food and drink and various ceremonial washings—external regulations applying until the time of the new order. (Hebrews 9:10)

Yesterday's passage reminds the Hebrew audience of the exacting requirements of the Old Testament, of the need for the annual sin sacrifices of animals, and of the veil that separates them from their Creator. They cannot approach him directly. They must remain at a forced distance.

But through the Holy Spirit they can connect these key parts of the old covenant with the saving work of Jesus through the new covenant. As long as the first tabernacle was still functioning, the veil that separated God's presence in the Most Holy Place separated him from the Hebrew people.

We can view this functioning of the first tabernacle in two ways. One is that because the tabernacle—and the temple that replaced it—still existed at the time the letter of Hebrews was written, the people couldn't directly approach God. They needed an intermediary. They needed a high priest to offer an annual *animal* sacrifice to appease God for their many sins, which separated them from him.

Yet we can also view the tabernacle/temple as a metaphor to reference the first covenant, which Jesus fulfills. Jesus offers himself as a *human* sacrifice for the people's sins. When he does this, the veil in the temple that separates the Holy Place from the Most Holy Place—that keeps the people from their Creator—tears in two. This symbolically shows that they now have direct access to their Father in heaven.

This veil serves as an illustration, showing them their separation from God. It's an Old Testament parable, if you will, revealing that the old covenant was a stop-gap measure, falling short of being able to fully clear the consciences of those who came to the temple to worship him.

The Old Testament specifications of the tabernacle, of worshiping God there, and of offering sacrifices are part of the many requirements our Lord gave Moses and the people. Along with them are a dizzying array of regulations about eating, drinking, and ceremonial cleansings that the people were expected to follow in their day-to-day living. (We see these throughout Leviticus 1–7, 11–20, and 23–27, and Deuteronomy 4–6 and 11–30).

Yet these are all external requirements, and they apply to the people under the old covenant. They don't address an internal perspective—matters of the heart and of conscience. To cover our inner being, the Hebrews need a new order. They need a new covenant. They need the saving work of Jesus to fulfill the old way (Matthew 5:17).

How should the veil in the temple being ripped in two inform our relationship with God? How have we wrongly let external requirements of the old covenant impact us today?

[Discover more about the work of the Holy Spirit throughout the letter to the Hebrews in Hebrews 2:4, 3:7–11, 6:4–5, 9:8, and 10:15–18.]

DAY 23: A CLEANSED CONSCIENCE
HEBREWS 9:11–15

How much more, then, will the blood of Christ, who through the eternal Spirit offered himself unblemished to God, cleanse our consciences. (Hebrews 9:14)

Yesterday we talked about Jesus coming as our new high priest to do away with the need for the annual animal sacrifices. He becomes our permanent human sacrifice. We see the results tangibly on earth when the veil in the temple that separates the Holy Place from the Most Holy Place—the one that keeps us from God—rips in two and gives us direct access to the Father.

Yet more significantly, Jesus—through his death —enters the original tabernacle in heaven. There he gives us direct access to the Father in the supernatural realm. What happens in the man-made tabernacle here on earth portrays what happens in the perfect tabernacle in heaven.

Jesus does not do this through the annual animal sacrifices prescribed under the old covenant. He does this by offering himself as a human sacrifice, a final and permanent solution. By dying—by giving his blood—he becomes the perfect sacrifice, thereby stopping the need for incomplete annual sacrifices.

The annual death of animals in the Old Testament for the people's wrongdoing reminds them of their sin. Though they are temporarily clean, it's only on the outside.

In contrast, Jesus cleanses us internally. Through him we have a clear conscience from our sins that deserve the punishment of death.

We often think of Jesus's salvation as providing us with eternal life. This is true, but there's more. Much more.

Jesus dies for us so that we may serve the living God.

Accepting Jesus's saving death merely to go to heaven when we die is shortsighted. Salvation through Jesus also applies to us here on earth now.

As his followers, we have a purpose in our world while we're alive.

We are to serve our Heavenly Father.

For us to serve Papa is why Jesus mediates God's new covenant. His death sets us free from the sins that the law of the first covenant reveals. Through the new covenant we'll receive an eternal inheritance—living forever with Jesus in heaven.

In what ways can we serve the living God here on earth today? Do we act as though Jesus has set us free from our sins?

[Discover what the letter to the Hebrews says about cleansing our consciences—that is, having a clear conscience—in Hebrews 9:9, 9:14, 10:22, and 13:18.]

DAY 24: THE FINAL SACRIFICE
HEBREWS 9:16–28

Christ was sacrificed once to take away the sins of many; and he will appear a second time, not to bear sin, but to bring salvation. (Hebrews 9:28)

We're not wrong to consider a covenant like a will. A will doesn't go into effect until after a death occurs. Under the old covenant this was the death of an animal. Under Jesus's new covenant it is *his* death. In both cases, death sets in motion what each covenant specifies.

As the old covenant required the spilling of blood, so too does the new one. Though the old covenant demanded an annual blood sacrifice of animals, the new covenant does not. As the perfect human sacrifice, Jesus's death ended the need for ongoing animal sacrifices that only temporarily cleansed the people of their sins.

The writers of Hebrews remind us that Jesus doesn't enter the earthly replica of the tabernacle when he dies. Instead, he enters heaven itself, into God's very presence. In addition, Jesus doesn't need to do this over and over, as did the high priests under the old covenant. Jesus suffers and dies one time. Once is enough. Jesus's death is the final sacrifice to remove the sins of all people throughout all time.

In this way Jesus comes to earth to die once, removing the sins of many. And he will appear a second time, not to die again, but to bring salvation to those who await him with expectation.

We can interpret this second appearance of Jesus in multiple ways. Here are two thoughts.

Just as he ascended into heaven after he rose from the dead, he will one day descend from heaven and return to earth (Acts 1:10–11). Then he will gather his followers and take them to be with him forever (John 14:2–3).

This will complete his saving work. This promise, however, doesn't apply to every believer, but only to those living when he returns. Those who died prior to his second coming will already be with him.

Another understanding of his second appearance is to compare this with the high priest's annual duty under the old covenant. The people see the high priest enter the Most Holy Place to offer the annual sacrifice. But they can't see what he's doing. They don't know when he finishes.

Instead, they wait outside for the high priest to emerge from the Most Holy Place. Only when they see him a second time do they know the sacrifice has been completed. Then they can have assurance their sins are covered—for one more year.

In the same way as these Old Testament high priests, Jesus appears a second time to confirm the sacrifice has been completed. His death represents the final sacrifice, the sacrifice to end them all.

Though this second explanation may not mean much to us today, the Hebrew people of old would have certainly grasped the connection. It would comfort them, tying the old covenant that they know well with Jesus's new covenant that they're just beginning to embrace.

Are we awaiting Jesus's return with eager expectation? What will he find us doing when he returns a second time?

[Discover a parallel story about another priest serving in the temple, offering the daily burning of incense, in Luke 1:8–22.]

DAY 25: WHAT THE LAW FORESHADOWS

HEBREWS 10:1–9

The law is only a shadow of the good things that are coming —not the realities themselves. (Hebrews 10:1)

The book of Hebrews talks a lot about the law, as revealed in the old covenant. A key part of the law, which we've covered in depth, is the animal sacrifice made year after year. But this sacrifice is only a shadow—a foretaste —of what is coming. The law shows we can look forward to perfection through Jesus.

These annual sacrifices remind people that they fall short of God's expectations. And this yearly offering of blood provides a degree of outward cleansing for the people to wash away their sins, albeit temporarily. Though this sacrifice offers cleansing, it does not remove sins. It's impossible for the blood of bulls and goats to do that.

The high priest must repeat the sin sacrifice every year, proving that it offers an incomplete solution. Otherwise, one sacrifice would be enough. That's why these sacrifices foreshadow the good things to come. What are these positive outcomes the law hints at? It's being made right with Papa through Jesus's death.

More to the point, the writers of Hebrews say Jesus's death for our sins makes us perfect. Since Jesus has died once, thereby forgiving everyone throughout all time of all their sins—of all *our* sins —there is no need to repeat it. It's one and done.

If Jesus needed to die a second time, that would confirm that the first time was inadequate—just as with the annual animal sacrifices. Yet Jesus offers the final sacrifice—the ultimate human sacrifice— to save everyone once and for all. In doing so he makes us perfect in God's sight.

We see this foretold in the Old Testament. In his plaintive psalm, David taps into the heart of God. He says God doesn't want sacrifices and burnt offerings for sins (Psalm 40:6–8). It's interesting that God proclaims this even though the law requires it—and he gave the law to Moses.

David foretells the words of Jesus when he writes, Here I am. I will accomplish what the prophets wrote about me and do your will, for your law is written on my heart. Though none of the four biographies of Jesus record him quoting these Old Testament words, the writers of Hebrews confirm he did.

Jesus comes to do his Father's will (Matthew 26:39 and Luke 22:42). In doing so, he makes us perfect.

What do we think about Jesus making us perfect? How should Jesus's once-and-for-all sacrifice change how we think and act?

[Discover what else God says in the Old Testament about sacrifices in 1 Samuel 15:22, Psalm 51:16, Jeremiah 7:21–23, and Hosea 6:6.]

DAY 26: MADE HOLY
HEBREWS 10:10–17

And by that will, we have been made holy through the sacrifice of the body of Jesus Christ once for all. (Hebrews 10:10)

Today's passage opens by referring to a will. We covered the need for a will in Day 24: "The Final Sacrifice." And we read about it in Hebrews 9:16–17. We likened a will to a covenant, which required a death to put the contents of a will—that is, the purpose of a covenant—into place.

The old covenant did this through animal sacrifices made year after year. The death of these animals resulted in an imperfect solution to the problem of sin. This is what the old covenant—the will—specifies.

Yet the will of the new covenant makes us holy through the sacrificial death of Jesus once and for all. He provides a perfect solution to the problem of sin. Through his death he makes us holy. He makes us perfect. This is what the new covenant—the will —specifies.

The idea of being made holy is a challenging concept for me to accept. I suspect it's a struggle for many. Even more difficult is the idea that Jesus has made me perfect. Most days I feel far from being holy, even more so from being perfect. I suppose most followers of Jesus feel this way, even though the Bible teaches us differently.

Fortunately, God doesn't rely on our perceptions of being holy or perfect. He has a different standard. His standard comes through Jesus. Through the Savior's death—his singular sacrifice —he cleanses our sins and forgives them. In doing so he makes us right with Father God *and* reconciles us back into relationship with him.

Though the Old Testament talks a lot about the old covenant, it also mentions a new covenant that God will give to replace the old one. Speaking through the Holy Spirit, Jeremiah looks forward to a time when God will make a new covenant with his people. He will be their God and they will be his people (Jeremiah 31:33). And the writers of Hebrews quote from this passage.

We see this fulfilled through Jesus. God will forgive our sins because of Jesus's sacrifice. Through Jesus they—and we—become holy. He makes us perfect.

How do we reconcile the truth that Jesus has made us holy and perfect with our perception of who we are today? How can we square what the Bible says—such as us being made holy and perfect—with how we feel?

[Discover more about being made perfect—which Hebrews mentions more than any other book in Scripture—in Hebrews 7:11, 7:18–19, 10:1, 11:39–40, and 12:22–24.]

BONUS CONTENT: FOREVER FORGIVEN

Where these have been forgiven, sacrifice for sin is no longer necessary. (Hebrews 10:18)

As yesterday's passage wraps up, the writers quote Jeremiah 31:34. In it the prophet looks forward to a time when God will forgive the people and remember their sins no more. That time is now.

Jesus forgives our sins and forgets them. Though we may remember them, our Heavenly Father does not. Our record with him is clean. This is not a result of anything we've done but what Jesus did.

Because Jesus forgives *and* forgets our sins, the

need for ongoing sin sacrifices is over. Jesus died once to forgive everyone, for everything, forever.

This means there's no longer a need for sacrifices. We are forever forgiven.

How can we let go of our past sins, which Jesus has forgiven and the Father has forgotten? Does it grieve Jesus when we wallow in guilt over sins he already died to free us from?

[Discover more about forgiveness in Psalm 130:4, Matthew 26:28, Acts 2:38, and Colossians 1:13–14.]

DAY 27: LET US
HEBREWS 10:19–25

Let us draw near to God with a sincere heart and with the full assurance that faith brings. (Hebrews 10:22)

Today's passage opens with a word that excites me, *therefore*. Recall that therefore is a linking word that connects the prior writing with what follows it. Here the preceding text talks about Jesus forgiving our sins.

Because of this—and since we have confidence to approach the Father through Jesus's blood, and since he is our great high priest in the house of God —we're encouraged to do three things.

Each one begins with the instruction of "let us . . ."

Here they are:

First, let us draw near to God. Recall that when Jesus died the veil in the temple here on earth—which is a shadow of the veil in the temple in heaven—ripped in two. This allows us the opportunity to approach the Father directly, to draw near to him.

With rare exceptions (such as Noah, Abraham, Moses, David, and the prophets) this is an unprecedented possibility. Yet through Jesus, it now becomes a reality for everyone. May we, therefore, draw near to God.

Second, let us cling to the hope we profess in Jesus. He is faithful to deliver what he promised (Hebrews 10:23). We'll talk more about this in our reading for Day 28.

Third, let us consider how we can urge one another to love better and help others (Hebrews 10:24). Implicitly we do this by not giving up meeting together (Hebrews 10:25).

God created us to live in community with others and with him. He didn't intend for us to be alone, to pursue life—and faith—in isolation. We need others to be at our finest, to thrive, and to best advance the kingdom of God.

Many people read this verse and assume the

writers of Hebrews are commanding us to go to church on Sunday. But the text doesn't say that. And we're wrong to assume it does. Though going to church *can* be one way to meet, it's not the only way. It may not even be the best way.

There are many options for how we can gather. We must contemplate how and be open to the Holy Spirit filling us with creative ideas. Then we must act. This may mean joining with others in their meetings or starting a gathering of our own.

The key is to form a habit of regularly gathering with other like-minded believers. And when we come together, we should encourage one another in our faith journey, loving others and doing good in the name of Jesus to advance his kingdom.

Aside from going to church on Sunday, what are other ways we can meet with followers of Jesus? What should we do to be more intentional about encouraging one another?

[Discover more about encouragement in Acts 15:32, Romans 1:11–12, 1 Corinthians 14:31, 2 Corinthians 13:11, and 1 Thessalonians 5:11, 14.]

BONUS CONTENT: DELIBERATE SIN

If we deliberately keep on sinning after we have received the knowledge of the truth, no sacrifice for sins is left. (Hebrews 10:26)

This verse about deliberate sin concerns many followers of Jesus. They look at their life and consider the sins they struggle with habitually or commit deliberately. They worry that their not-yet-resolved struggle may keep them from receiving Jesus's salvation.

Indeed, if we take this verse in isolation, we may reach that conclusion. Yet considering it in context results in a much different understanding—and removes our dread over what this passage means.

As we read on, the writers of Hebrews compare this thought to the people who rejected the law of Moses in the Old Testament, under the old covenant. They died without mercy.

So it is with the new covenant. Those who reject Jesus are enemies of God; they should expect judgment and fire. This is the deliberate sin. It occurs when people make a conscious decision to not follow Jesus.

But this verse does not apply to those of us who already follow him. For us, it's a nonissue—other than a reminder to warn others not to reject Jesus.

Have we taken the all-important step to follow Jesus? Who should we talk to about Jesus?

[Discover more about our sins in Acts 13:38–39, Ephesians 1:7, Hebrews 8:12, and 1 John 1:9.]

DAY 28: PERSEVERE
HEBREWS 10:26–39

You need to persevere so that when you have done the will of God, you will receive what he has promised. (Hebrews 10:36)

Today's passage opens with the imperative need for us to accept Jesus and follow him. In doing so we will have no reason to fear God's judgment and eternal fire.

Yet following Jesus is not without its own set of concerns. The writers of Hebrews list some struggles that Jesus's followers must deal with. In short, they will face oppression for being a Christian.

This includes public insult, persecution, imprisonment, or property confiscation for those who follow Jesus. There is also suffering for standing by those who face these struggles.

We see these things happen to the Hebrew Christians for their belief in Jesus. In many cases their persecution comes from fellow Hebrews. Consider what Paul does to Christians—that is, followers of the Way—prior to his encounter with Jesus on the road to Damascus (Acts 9:1–19).

Yet the persecution of Christians for their faith isn't only something that happened two thousand years ago. It still happens today.

Depending on where we live and our life circumstances, the impact is different.

Some read these items as something that could happen to them but hasn't. Others have had first-hand encounters in one of these areas. Still others face all these items every day. The text says they endure great conflict packed with suffering.

The writers of the letter to the Hebrews, however, don't tell them to ask God for deliverance from persecution. This isn't to say we shouldn't pray about it. We should, but we may not receive the deliverance we seek in this life. Even so, we must maintain our faith in Jesus.

So what should our reaction be? We must maintain the confidence that we place in Jesus. That is, to hold on to our faith amid persecution. When we do, we will receive a rich reward.

In short, we must persevere.

This is the will of God. And through our perseverance, we will receive his promise. He is coming soon, as revealed through prophecy and revelation (Habakkuk 2:3–4 and Revelation 22:20).

If we shrink back in the face of religious torment, we will face destruction. But if we persevere in faith, we will receive salvation.

Therefore, we must persevere.

How have we suffered for our faith? How can we encourage one another to persevere and not shrink back?

[Discover more about persecution in Romans 8:35, 2 Corinthians 12:10, 2 Timothy 3:10–11, and Revelation 2:10.]

DAY 29: BY FAITH
HEBREWS 11:1–7

Without faith it is impossible to please God, because anyone who comes to him must believe that he exists and that he rewards those who earnestly seek him. (Hebrews 11:6)

People often call Hebrews 11 the Bible's Hall of Fame, or more correctly, the Bible's Hall of *Faith*. It names sixteen Old Testament characters we can celebrate for their faith (and covers many more implicitly). The Hebrew followers of Jesus would have been very familiar with these individuals. Being reminded of their faith in the past encourages the Hebrews to persist in their newfound faith in Jesus.

In the same way, these faith-filled followers of God can encourage us today.

Hebrews 11 opens with a powerful description of faith: "Now faith is confidence in what we hope for and assurance about what we do not see" (verse 1). Memorize this verse. Meditate on it. It is key.

An example is that by faith we believe God formed our universe, speaking it into existence from what is unseen. By faith we accept that God made something from nothing, using the power of his spoken word to create us and our reality. As we accept our creation by faith, we likewise embrace our salvation through faith.

The first biblical character affirmed for his faith is Abel (Genesis 4:1–9). By faith Abel gives a better offering to God than his brother, Cain. This implies a lack of faith on Cain's part. Though the Genesis account doesn't mention Abel's faith, the letter to the Hebrews confirms it. What's interesting with this story is there is no record that God tells the brothers to give him their offerings; they just do. And Abel gives his offering in faith.

Next up is Enoch (Genesis 5:23–24). He walks with God in faith, and God takes him away. Imagine being spared death and God whisking Enoch away to be with him.

Noah is the third person of faith listed in this passage (Genesis 6–8). God alerts him of the flood that will come. In faith, Noah believes God about what will happen. He builds a giant boat. In doing so, he saves his family and all the animals on the ark.

Without faith—as exemplified by these three men of old—it's impossible to please God.

It is through faith that we believe he exists. It is through faith that he will reward those who seek him.

What part does faith play for those who follow Jesus? What does it take to have a faith that will please God?

[Discover more about another man who did not die and was taken up into heaven in 2 Kings 2:1–18.]

DAY 30: ABRAHAM
HEBREWS 11:8–12

By faith Abraham, when called to go to a place he would later receive as his inheritance, obeyed and went, even though he did not know where he was going. (Hebrews 11:8)

As we move through our biblical timeline in Hebrews 11, next up is Father Abraham. His faith-filled exploits provide us with a model to follow. Although Abraham also made some foolish mistakes, this doesn't take away from his deep faith that God affirms and the writers of Hebrews celebrate.

God comes to Abraham—first called Abram—when he lives far away in a pagan culture. In what is the first record in Scripture of any interaction between them, God tells Abraham to move (Genesis 12:1–7). Once there, Abraham will receive an inheritance.

God doesn't say where to go, only that he will reveal the location later. The destination is on a need-to-know basis, and God doesn't think Abraham needs to know—yet.

To his credit, Abraham obeys. He heads out, traveling a long distance to the west, far away from his home, from his family, and from all he knows.

God leads him to the land of Canaan, the promised land. There Abraham settles. He lives in tents—like a nomad—a stranger in a foreign land. In faith, he looks forward to something better.

It's there when God promises to make Abraham into a great nation, even though he and his wife, Sarah, are old and childless. Abraham accepts God's promise in faith, as does Sarah, despite the fact that she's well past her childbearing years.

Later, God expands his promise to Abraham. The Almighty replaces his pledge to make Abraham's descendants into *a* nation, by saying that *many* nations will come from him (Genesis 17:5).

And because Abraham and Sarah believe in faith what God promised, they have a son in their old age (Genesis 21:1–7). Abraham's descendants will be as numerous as the stars.

We'll soon read another story of Abraham's faith when God tells him to sacrifice his only son, Isaac. Although God ends up not requiring Abraham to follow through, Abraham is willing to kill Isaac in faith, believing that God can raise him from the dead.

Which of Abraham's steps of faith most inspires us? When God tells us to do something do we say yes or ask questions?

[Discover more about Abraham's faith in Romans 4:1–25 and Galatians 3:6–9.]

DAY 31: LIVING IN FAITH
HEBREWS 11:13–16

All these people were still living by faith when they died.
(Hebrews 11:13)

S o far in Hebrews chapter 11 we've talked about the faith of Abel, Enoch, and Noah. We explored the faith of Abraham, along with his wife Sarah, whose faith extends to their offspring Isaac and Jacob. And we will talk about many more people of faith in the rest of Hebrews 11.

All these pillars of faith—notable examples for us to emulate—lived in expectation of what was to come. And they were still living by faith when they died, having not yet received what God had promised. They persisted to the end in their belief about what was to be. They finished their life strong, even though they didn't realize what God had pledged to give them.

Yet this does not mean their faith was in vain.

To the contrary, their perseverance proves how strong their faith was. They persisted in faith to the ends of their lives despite never receiving what they lived in expectation to see. Instead, they only saw God's promise from a distance. They received what was to come in faith.

They saw themselves as foreigners on earth—aliens—and strangers (see Genesis 23:4). Though they lived here, they didn't belong here. And neither do we. Just as they were aliens, so are we.

These people of faith looked forward to a place of their own, their own country, a *better* country. This better country loomed before them not as a physical place, but as a supernatural one—a heavenly destination.

Because of their faith, God is happy to be their God. And because of their faith he has prepared a place for them, a city where they will live with him eternally.

By faith in God and his promises, they anticipated heaven. Though they did this through what was to come for them, we do so by what has already come for us: Jesus.

Do we perceive ourselves as foreigners and strangers here on earth? Are we by faith looking forward to a better country, a heavenly one?

[Discover more about Jesus preparing a place for us in John 14:2–3 and read about God's city, the new Jerusalem, where his people will live with him forever, in Revelation 21:2.]

BONUS CONTENT: HEBREWS HALL OF FAITH

They were longing for a better country—a heavenly one.
(Hebrews 11:16)

Here's a list of the characters of faith mentioned in Hebrews 11, along with key passages about them.

- Abel (Genesis 4:1–9)
- Enoch (Genesis 5:21–24)
- Noah (Genesis 6–8)
- Abraham (Genesis 12:1–7 and Genesis 22:1–19)
- Sarah (Genesis 21:1–7)
- Isaac (Genesis 27:1–40)

- Jacob (Genesis 48:8–22)
- Joseph (Genesis 50:24–26)
- Moses's parents (Exodus 2:1–10)
- Moses (Exodus 12:1–30 and Exodus 14:21–31)
- Rahab (Joshua 2:1–24 and Joshua 6:1–25)
- Gideon (Judges 7:2–15)
- Barak (Judges 4:4–24)
- Samson (Judges 16:26–30)
- Jephthah (Judges 11:29–33)
- David (1 Samuel 13:14, confirmed in Acts 13:22)
- Samuel (Psalm 99:6)

The prophets (mostly in the books of Isaiah through Malachi, but also scattered throughout the rest of the Old Testament)

Which of these Bible characters do you most relate to? Who do you know who's a person of faith?

[Discover more about faith in James 2:14–26, 1 Peter 1:3–9, and Jude 1:3.]

DAY 32: ISAAC, JACOB, AND JOSEPH
HEBREWS 11:17–23

By faith Joseph, when his end was near, spoke about the exodus of the Israelites from Egypt and gave instructions concerning the burial of his bones. (Hebrews 11:22)

Having celebrated the faith of some patriarchs and applauded them for what they only saw from afar, let's look at some more like-minded people of faith. But first we'll revisit Abraham.

As we alluded to in Day 30: "Abraham," there's an incident with him and his son Isaac. Though Abraham had other children both before and after Isaac (Genesis 16 and 25:1–6), Isaac is the only child of Abraham and Sarah. In a test of

Abraham's faith, God tells him to offer Isaac as a burnt offering, a human sacrifice (Genesis 22:1–19). Though this surely vexes him, Abraham agrees to do just that—even though God's promises to Abraham were supposed to flow through Isaac.

Abraham prepares the altar, lays wood on it, and places a bound Isaac on top. With knife lifted and ready to plunge into his son, God stops Abraham from following through. Abraham's willingness to obey God confirms his faith. He even believes the Almighty would raise Isaac from the dead. Effectively that's what happens.

It's interesting to note that Isaac is a direct ancestor of Jesus (Matthew 1:2–16). Had Isaac died without offspring, Jesus couldn't have been born—at least not through the bloodline we read in the New Testament. In this story of Isaac, we also see him nearly becoming a human sacrifice. This foreshadows his descendant Jesus, who does, in fact, become a human sacrifice when he dies for our sins.

Later, by faith, Isaac blesses his two sons, Jacob and Esau, prophetically proclaiming their future (Genesis 27:1–40).

By faith, Jacob blesses two of his grandsons—Joseph's boys—before he dies (Genesis 48:8–22).

Abraham, Isaac, and Jacob are all Jesus's direct ancestors.

As his life nears its end, by faith Joseph instructs the people to carry his bones out of Egypt to the land God gave to Abraham (Genesis 50:24–26). And four centuries later, Joshua does exactly that (Joshua 24:32).

But before Joshua, there was Moses. Moses's parents see their son as unique and, by faith in God, they resist the Egyptian king's decree and hide their son for three months (Exodus 2:1–10). In this way they protect him from the pharaoh's edict to kill all Israelite baby boys. This ensures that Moses lives long enough to lead the people out of Egypt.

In what ways does the faith of these people encourage and inspire us today? Whether we have physical offspring or spiritual offspring, what can we do to best prepare them for the future God has planned for them?

[Discover more about Moses's rescue from certain death in Exodus 2:1–10.]

DAY 33: MOSES
HEBREWS 11:24–31

By faith Moses, when he had grown up, refused to be known as the son of Pharaoh's daughter. (Hebrews 11:24)

We covered Moses's parents who, by faith in God, do not fear the pharaoh. They take steps to save their baby boy from certain death. Their actions, which are driven by their faith, ensure their son can live and become who God wants him to be.

By faith, Moses chooses not to live in the palace as a son of the pharaoh's daughter. Instead, he aligns with his own people. Though we applaud him for the faith to do so, we wonder how he developed such a godly confidence. Surely his adopted

Egyptian family did not teach him about his heritage, of the faith of Abraham, Isaac, and Jacob.

We know the pharaoh's daughter hires Moses's mom to nurse him—though unaware she's his biological mother (Exodus 2:7).

We wonder if Moses's mom continues to interact with him as he grows older and teaches him what she and their people believe. Regardless, Moses develops a strong faith in God. He sets aside the luxury of the pharaoh's palace and all the benefits he has by living there, dismissing them for his future reward.

By faith Moses stands up to the king—his adoptive grandfather—persevering to do what God tells him to do. In obedience he institutes the Passover, thereby saving the firstborn child of every Israelite family (Exodus 12:1–30).

Then Moses leads the people out of Egypt. By faith they cross the Red Sea on dry ground, but the Egyptians drown when they try to follow (Exodus 14:21–31). Whether it's by Moses's faith alone or that of the Israelites as a whole, God does save them.

Moses leads the people to the promised land, but he cannot enter it. This task falls to his protégé, Joshua. By faith, the walls of Jericho fall, and the people conquer the city, destroying everything and killing everyone—all except for the prostitute Rahab and her family. By faith, Rahab is spared (Joshua 6:1–25).

In another delightful note, we see that Rahab is an ancestor of King David and of Jesus. Rahab marries Salmon. They have Boaz. Boaz marries Ruth (who, like Rahab, is also not Jewish) and they have Obed. Obed is the father of Jesse, the father of King David (Matthew 1:5–6).

How should we react knowing that a prostitute has a faith that saves her from death? What do we think about a prostitute being in Jesus's family tree?

[Discover more about Ruth, a Moabite, another unlikely woman in Jesus's family tree in the book of Ruth.]

DAY 34: MORE EXAMPLES OF FAITH
HEBREWS 11:32–40

These were all commended for their faith, yet none of them received what had been promised. (Hebrews 11:39)

The writers of Hebrews have already compiled a notable list of Old Testament characters celebrated for their faith. But there are more. While they're only mentioned by name, this isn't because they're insignificant, but because of the time and space needed to cover them. Besides, the Hebrew audience would know them well.

First up is Gideon. Gideon is a reluctant hero, a judge in the time before Israel had a king. Though Gideon at first exhibits a lack of faith, he ends up boldly going in confidence that God will provide him with victory. Indeed, his small band of three hundred—along with God's provisions—defeats the entire Midianite army (Judges 6–8).

Another Old Testament character that we might dismiss is Barak. His story intertwines with Judge Deborah. She gives him God's command to lead an army of 10,000 against their enemy. Then God will grant him victory. Barak agrees, but only if Deborah goes with him. They are victorious (Judges 4:4–24).

Next up is Samson. We know him best for his relationship with Delilah, which brings about his downfall. Disobedience marks most of Samson's life, but in the end, he places his faith in God and brings about the death of more than 3,000 Philistines (Judges 13–16).

Jephthah emerges as a military leader despite a less-than-ideal beginning and his people's initial rejection of him. Before going into battle, he promises to sacrifice to God the first thing he sees when he returns victorious. When he comes back his daughter greets him, much to his dismay. Though he made a foolish vow, he had faith God would grant him victory (Judges 11:30–39).

King David is a biblical character we know

much about. Though he has many shortcomings, God proclaims him "a man after his own heart" (1 Samuel 13:14 and Acts 13:22). This is something that can only come about through a steadfast faith in God.

Next, we have the prophet Samuel. He lives during the time of Kings Saul and David. In faith, he serves God and obeys what God tells him to do (1 Samuel 7–19).

Last are the prophets. Many have books in the Bible named after them, while others do not. We know some well, but others are more obscure. What they all have in common is that by faith they heed God's call to be his prophet, they proclaim his words to the people, and they trust him with the outcome.

The book of Hebrews commends all these people mentioned in Chapter 11 for their faith. Yet none of them live long enough to receive what God had promised. He has something better in mind for them—and for us.

It is through Jesus. And through him—by faith—we can all become perfect (Hebrews 11:40).

How can the lives of these biblical characters encourage us in our faith? What do we think about Jesus making us perfect?

[Discover more about being perfect in Matthew 5:48, 2 Corinthians 7:1, and James 3:2, as well as throughout the book of Hebrews.]

DAY 35: RUN WITH PERSEVERANCE
HEBREWS 12:1–3

Let us run with perseverance the race marked out for us, fixing our eyes on Jesus, the pioneer and perfecter of faith.
(Hebrews 12:1–2)

Today's focus verse provides this book's title: *Run with Perseverance.* But before we get to that we need to start with the beginning of this passage. It opens with the word *therefore,* connecting what follows it with what precedes it. In this case it's our Hebrews 11 Hall of Faith.

It provides us with the imagery of a great cloud of witnesses surrounding us, the people of note-worthy faith we've just read about. We can interpret their witness in two ways. One is that their lives serve as a witness to us. The other is that they are witnessing *our* lives. Imagine these Old Testament saints watching us and cheering us on in our journey of faith. It's a heady thought. May we find encouragement in it.

Because of their example and their witness, the writers of Hebrews encourage us to do two things. Both begin with the inspiring instruction of "let us."

First, let us throw off everything that holds us back, to jettison each weight that slows us down. This includes the entanglement of sin. If we wrongly hold on to these things, it does not negate our right standing with Jesus, but it does affect how we live our lives while we're here on earth and the reward we'll receive once we leave this place. Remember, we have an impressive throng of witnesses cheering us on.

Second, let us run with perseverance the race before us. Having ridden ourselves of all the baggage that would slow us down, we're ready to run. We're poised to speed down the path God has for us. As we do, we want to keep our focus on Jesus, to maintain a steady gaze on him. He is the reason for our faith and the perfecter of it.

Jesus now sits in heaven at God's right hand.

He, too, is our witness. His life and sacrifice serve as a witness to us. And, from the vantage point of heaven, he witnesses what we're doing with this new life that he gave us.

If the patriarchs' witness motivates us to move forward in faith, how much more should Jesus's witness? He endured for us, which should encourage us to persevere for him, to not grow weary or lose heart.

We must, therefore, run our race with perseverance.

How can we best run our race with perseverance? How can Jesus and the great cloud of witnesses encourage us in our faith journey?

[Discover more about perseverance in Romans 5:1–4, James 1:2–4, and 2 Peter 1:5–7.]

BONUS CONTENT: OUR STRUGGLE AGAINST SIN

In your struggle against sin, you have not yet resisted to the point of shedding your blood. (Hebrews 12:4)

We already talked about how Jesus can help us with temptation. (See the Bonus Content: "Help When Tempted," which is based on Hebrews 2:18.)

We now encounter the topic of sin again in the book of Hebrews. It acknowledges that we struggle with sin. More to the point, we struggle *against* sin. And it reminds us that Jesus also faced sin and had to resist it. He did this to the point of shedding his blood.

We can look at this in two ways. Both have merit.

The first and obvious one is that when Jesus dies on the cross, he becomes a sin sacrifice to bear on himself—at that moment—the weight of all sins, for all people, throughout all time. And we know he struggles with this because he asks God to take this burden from him (Luke 22:42). But his mission is to die for us, and Jesus does just that, deferring to his Father's will. We get the full impact of his agony when he cries out to God, "Why have you forsaken me?" (Mark 15:34).

The second is indirect, yet also insightful. As Jesus seeks his Father in prayer prior to his execution, his sweat falls like drops of blood (Luke 22:44). Though most versions stop short of saying Jesus bled as he prayed, The Living Bible (TLB) is direct: "he was in such agony of spirit that he broke into a sweat of blood." Regardless, we understand the gravity of his prayers. If he struggled in prayer to deal with our sins, this should encourage us to struggle in prayer against our temptation to sin.

Although we want to live holy lives in response to Jesus dying for our sins, we must remember that he doesn't require us to be sinless to save us. We receive our salvation by grace through faith

(Ephesians 2:8). When we accept Jesus, he washes away our sins (Acts 22:16).

How can Jesus's struggle encourage us today? How can we best fight against sin?

[Discover more about sin and grace in Romans 6:1–2 and Ephesians 1:7.]

DAY 36: DISCIPLINE THROUGH HARDSHIP

HEBREWS 12:5–13

Endure hardship as discipline; God is treating you as his children. (Hebrews 12:7)

The book of Hebrews moves from the encouragement to run our race with perseverance—looking to Jesus in our struggle with sin—to the subject of discipline. Consider how these three ideas might connect.

In looking specifically at discipline, the text doesn't address self-discipline. Instead, it looks at discipline as administered by Father God.

Our discipline comes in the form of hardship.

We should endure these difficulties, viewing them as our heavenly Father's discipline to us—to his children—whom he loves. No one wants hardship in their life, and most want to avoid discipline. Yet godly discipline is good for us. We should accept it as an act of love because that's what it is.

We are children of God. As his children, he disciplines us for our own good, just as any human parent disciplines their child.

Though people do not always correct their children with perfect precision, our Heavenly Father's discipline to us is without fault. Yes, we may not always understand his discipline—as seen through the hardships we face—but we can always trust him with it.

When we receive his discipline, we should accept it and thank him for it. His discipline is painful, yet it produces results in us and moves us toward holiness.

But what does it mean if we're not seeing our heavenly Father's discipline in our lives?

From this text we might see only two conclusions. The first is that we're already living a most holy life and need no more correction. Though possible, it's also doubtful. The other reason is that God doesn't view us as his children, as his true sons and daughters. Therefore, he sees no need to discipline us.

We can also consider a third possibility.

This comes to us from Hebrews 5:11–14, which we covered in Day 12: "Time to Teach." It's about those who are infants in Christ, needing milk and unable to handle solid food.

A parent would never discipline a baby—because an infant doesn't know any better. So it is with our Heavenly Father. He won't discipline us if we're not mature enough.

And just as a wise parent adjusts their discipline as their child moves from being a baby to a toddler, to a preteen, to a teenager, so too does God adjust his discipline of us based on our maturity level.

If we follow Jesus and are a child of God, we should receive his discipline. And if we're not, it suggests we aren't mature enough to handle it, that we're still a baby Christian.

But for those of us who are more mature in our faith, we should receive Papa's discipline as his affirmation. It shows he loves us and proves he wants us to grow in our faith.

The result is holiness and a harvest of righteousness and peace.

What do we think about God's discipline to us coming in the form of hardship? How can we best endure the hardships we face as God disciplines us?

[Discover more about hardship in Acts 20:23, Romans 8:35, 2 Corinthians 12:10, and 2 Timothy 4:5.]

DAY 37: LIVE AT PEACE
HEBREWS 12:14–17

Make every effort to live in peace with everyone and to be holy. (Hebrews 12:14)

The Hebrews text says we are to make every effort to live at peace with everyone. It doesn't say make *some* effort. It doesn't say make *a little* effort. And it doesn't say try until it gets too hard. It says *every* effort.

Paul tells the church in Rome the same thing (Romans 12:18).

In this way we are called to be peacemakers. Jesus says that peacemakers will receive God's blessings and that they are children of God (Matthew

5:9). And James writes that peacemakers who sow peace will reap righteousness (James 3:18).

We will, therefore, do well to make every effort to live at peace with everyone.

But there's more.

Our focus verse contains the conjunction *and*. Not only must we make every effort to live in peace, but we must also make every effort to be holy.

Living in peace reflects our relationship with others, whereas being holy reflects our relationship with God.

We get a hint of how to be holy in the verses that follow this instruction. We are to see that no one falls short of God's grace, we are to see that bitterness does not grow in us, we are to see that we avoid sexual immorality, and we are to see that we avoid godlessness.

Holiness is something Papa desires, and holiness is something we pursue in response to what Jesus did for us when he died to make us right with our Father in heaven. Though we don't need to live a holy life to get God's attention and earn his favor, pursuing a holy lifestyle should be a heartfelt outgrowth of our love for him.

Recall yesterday's reading, Day 37: "Discipline through Hardship," where one result of God's discipline—of enduring hardship—is to move us toward holiness.

Holy is a reoccurring word in the book of Hebrews, appearing in nineteen verses, more than any other book in the New Testament, aside from Acts.

The idea of holy living is something the Hebrew audience would know well. The purpose of the Old Testament law is to show how to live holy lives. Yet this also proves to be impossible; everyone falls short. Following a list of rules does not bring them—or us—into the holy status Father God desires.

Yet through Jesus we become holy. He forgives us and makes us holy, a lofty standard we can't achieve on our own. What a relief this must be for the Hebrews to know that Jesus makes them holy and makes them right with Papa. It's an outcome they could never achieve without him.

So it is when we follow Jesus and believe in him as our Savior.

In a spiritual sense, Jesus has already made us holy. Yet, in a physical sense, we have an opportunity—through Jesus—to become more holy in how we live our lives.

What should we do to make every effort to live at peace with everyone? What should we do to make every effort to be holy?

[Discover more about living in peace in Isaiah 32:17–18, 2 Corinthians 13:11, and 1 Thessalonians 5:13.]

DAY 38: THE TALE OF TWO MOUNTAINS

HEBREWS 12:18–29

But you have come to Mount Zion, to the city of the living God, the heavenly Jerusalem. (Hebrews 12:22)

Today's text talks about two mountains: one mountain experience that *was*, and one mountain experience that *will be*. We read about that first mountain—Mount Sinai—in the Old Testament. What happens on this mountain is the foundation of the Hebrew people's faith.

This is where and when God gives Moses the Ten Commandments and his rules for right living. It is this covenant—sometimes called the Mosaic covenant—that the people live under as they await God's promise of something better.

Two months after the people escape Egypt, they reach the Sinai desert. They camp there, at the foot of Mount Sinai (Exodus 19:1–20:21).

God tells them not to approach the mountain or touch it. Anyone who does must die. From the base of the mountain, they will hear God speak to them through a dense cloud. The people consecrate themselves to hear from God on the third day.

On that day, Moses leads the people to the base of the mountain. Thunder booms and lightning flashes. A trumpet blasts and everyone trembles. God descends on the mountain with fire; smoke billows like from a furnace. The mountain shakes. The trumpet wail swells, and at last God speaks.

Fear grips the people, and they tremble. They beg God to speak to Moses instead of directly to them. So God gives the people his laws and expectations through Moses. These events at Mount Sinai are the basis for the Hebrew faith.

Through Jesus, we come to a different mountain. This is not a mountain that gives us rules to follow and obey, like Mount Sinai. Instead, it's a mountain that represents God's grace to us through Jesus. It is Mount Zion, a new Jerusalem in heavenly form. It's where God lives, and the angels assemble.

And it's where we will live with God under his new covenant made with us through Jesus. Jesus will mediate this new covenant, one sprinkled with blood—as foreshadowed through the old covenant with Moses—to cleanse us and make us right with Father God.

God shook the earth at Mount Sinai when he gave Moses his laws. This time he shakes the earth —and heaven along with it—a final time to give us Jesus and salvation through him.

How would we react if we were at the base of Mount Sinai and heard the voice of God? What do we most anticipate about our future in Mount Zion?

[Discover more about Mount Zion in Revelation 14:1 and the heavenly Jerusalem in Revelation 21:1–8.]

BONUS CONTENT: AN UNSHAKABLE KINGDOM

Therefore, since we are receiving a kingdom that cannot be shaken, let us be thankful, and so worship God acceptably with reverence and awe. (Hebrews 12:28)

The passage preceding today's verse, which connects with the lovely word *therefore*, talks about the two mountains. Mount Sinai was shaken. Mount Zion will result from God once more shaking things up on earth and in heaven. But it's the final shake-up.

This last shaking will remove the shakable Mount Sinai. In its place will emerge an unshakable Mount Zion. As a result, it will remain an eternal home for us forever. This is the kingdom we will receive when we put our faith in Jesus.

Therefore, we should receive this kingdom with thanksgiving. We should also worship God. We do this with reverence and awe.

He is our consuming fire.

Though the phrase *consuming fire* only appears once in the New Testament, in Hebrews 12:29, it shows up several times in the Old Testament. We first see it when God confirms his covenant with Moses and the people (Exodus 24:17). At that time, the Lord's glory looked like a consuming fire on top of Mount Sinai. We see this reference to consuming fire as judgment to those people who don't obey the laws God gives to them through Moses.

And God will be our consuming fire now if we reject him (see Hebrews 10:29–31). Yet Mount Zion awaits those who believe in Jesus and follow him. There we will bask in his glory, but it won't be a consuming fire of judgment.

How can we worship God with reverence and awe? How do we react to God as our consuming fire?

[Discover more about consuming fire in Deuteronomy 4:24, 2 Samuel 22:9, Psalm 18:8, Isaiah 30:27–33, and Isaiah 33:14.]

DAY 39: MADE HOLY
HEBREWS 13:1–14

And so Jesus also suffered outside the city gate to make the people holy through his own blood. (Hebrews 13:12)

The last chapter of Hebrews wraps up with a list of commands. These are exhortations for the Hebrew people who follow Jesus—and for us. Here are the key calls to action we see in Hebrews 13:

- Keep on loving each other (verse 1).
- Show hospitality to strangers (verse 2).
- Remember those in prison as if we were there with them (verse 3).

- Honor marriage and keep it pure; no adultery or sexual immorality (verse 4).
- Avoid greed and be content with what we have (verse 5).
- Remember our spiritual leaders (verse 7) and pray for them (verse 18).
- Be wary of strange teachings (verse 9).
- Be strengthened by grace and not by following rituals (verse 9).
- Do good and share with others (verse 16).
- Obey our leaders and submit to their authority (verse 17).

Mixed in with these commands are other truths and encouragements. First is a reminder that God will always be with us (verse 5, which quotes Deuteronomy 31:6). Next is that God is our helper, and we have nothing to fear from what people can do to us (verse 6, which quotes Psalm 118:6–7).

We also have a teaching that Jesus doesn't change. He's the same yesterday, today, and forever (verse 8, which references God in Psalm 55:19).

After this, the writers of Hebrews slip in one more teaching, as if to make sure we don't miss it. It again connects Jesus with the Old Testament. Among the many rituals described in the book of Leviticus are instructions about the sin offerings.

Once the animal dies for the sin offering, its blood is brought into the Most Holy Place to make atonement for sins. Then the animal's body is taken outside the camp and burned (Leviticus 4:21 and Leviticus 16:27). The Hebrew people will be well acquainted with this process, witnessing it repeat annually, year after year.

In the same way, Jesus's blood is brought into the Most Holy Place, symbolically shown when the veil of the temple rips in two. Then his body is taken outside the camp—that is, outside the city. Though his body isn't burned, it is buried.

In doing so, he makes his people holy.

We go to Jesus's body outside the camp, outside the city. There we do not have a city to live in, but we look forward to the city that is to come, the new Jerusalem (Revelation 21:2).

Those of us who follow Jesus will spend eternity with him there.

How do we respond, knowing that Jesus's death makes us holy? Though we look forward to spending eternity with

Jesus, what can we do for him now while we're here on earth?

[Discover more about Jesus making us holy in Hebrews 2:11, 10:10, and 10:14.]

DAY 40: A SACRIFICE OF PRAISE
HEBREWS 13:15–25

Through Jesus, therefore, let us continually offer to God a sacrifice of praise—the fruit of lips that openly profess his name. (Hebrews 13:15)

As we wrap up the book of Hebrews, we look at the last half of its closing chapter, chapter 13. There are three key passages to focus on.

First, this section opens with the instruction to offer God a continual sacrifice of praise. We do this through Jesus—and only through Jesus.

The Old Testament Hebrew people needed to continually offer sin sacrifices—year after year—to cover for their sins, albeit partially. But we no longer need to do this. Jesus offered the final sin sacrifice that anyone would ever need. Therefore, the need to offer continuous sin sacrifices ended with Jesus.

Yet in response to what Jesus did for us, we can—we should—continually offer God a sacrifice of praise. But this "sacrifice" is no hardship. It's a privilege to thank Father God for what he did for us through Jesus. We do this when we openly profess his name.

The idea of calling it a sacrifice—a continual sacrifice—reminds us that the need for continual sin sacrifices is past, replaced with our continual offerings of praise to God.

In this way the letter's Hebrew audience will have one last chance to see how Jesus fulfills the Old Testament, just as he said he would (Matthew 5:17).

Second, let's consider the letter's benediction. What a powerful blessing it is. I've heard it at the end of church services, and its words flow lyrically. Here's a breakdown, paraphrased to cause us to slow down and better grasp its full impact:

May God equip us with all we need to do his will. May he work through us to accomplish what pleases him. We can do this through Jesus who receives all glory forever. Jesus's death and resurrection stands as an eternal covenant, with Jesus as our great Shepherd and we as his sheep.

The third and final phrase to point out in this concluding passage in the letter to the Hebrew Christians is a fitting farewell. This last sentence is simply "grace be with you all."

This mention of God's grace reminds us that Jesus saves us through grace and grace alone. We don't have to earn it—as the old covenant, in the Old Testament, requires. In fact, we *can't* earn it. We need merely to receive it, through no merit of our own. That's what grace means.

Thank you, Jesus, for loving us, dying for us, and forgiving our sins. When we put our faith in you, you make us right with Papa.

In what ways can we offer a continual sacrifice of praise to God? What must we do to remember that it's through God's grace we're made right?

[Discover more about grace in Romans 3:22–24, Galatians 2:21, Ephesians 2:8–9, and Revelation 22:21.]

If you liked *Hebrews Bible Study*, please leave a review online. Your review will help others discover this book and encourage them to read it too. Thank you.

WHAT BOOK DO YOU WANT TO READ NEXT?

Consider these other books in the 40-Day Bible Study Series:

- Dear Theophilus (the Gospel of Luke, formerly That You May Know)
- Acts Bible Study (formerly Tongues of Fire)
- Isaiah Bible Study (formerly For Unto Us)
- Minor Prophets Bible Study (formerly Return to Me)
- Job Bible Study (formerly I Hope in Him)
- Living Water (John)
- Love Is Patient (1 and 2 Corinthians)

- Revelation Bible Study
- 1, 2, & 3 John Bible Study (formerly Love One Another)
- James and Jude Bible Study
- Matthew Bible Study
- 1 & 2 Peter Bible Study
- Mark Bible Study

FOR SMALL GROUPS, SUNDAY SCHOOL, AND CLASSROOMS

Hebrews Bible Study makes an ideal eight-week Bible study discussion guide for small groups, Sunday School, and classes. To prepare for the conversation, read one chapter of this book each weekday, Monday through Friday.

- Week 1: read 1 through 5.
- Week 2: read 6 through 10.
- Week 3: read 11 through 15.
- Week 4: read 16 through 20.
- Week 5: read 21 through 25.
- Week 6: read 26 through 30.
- Week 7: read 31 through 35.
- Week 8: read 36 through 40.

When you get together, discuss the questions at the end of each chapter. The leader can use all the questions to guide this discussion or pick which ones to focus on.

Before beginning the discussion, pray as a group. Ask for Holy Spirit insight and clarity.

As you consider each chapter's questions:

- Look for how this can grow your understanding of the Bible.
- Evaluate how this can expand your faith perspective.
- Consider what you need to change in how you live your lives.

End by asking God to help apply what you've learned.

May God bless you as you read and study his Word.

IF YOU'RE NEW TO THE BIBLE

Each entry in this book contains Bible references. These can guide you if you want to learn more. If you're not familiar with the Bible, here's an overview to get you started, give some context, and minimize confusion.

First, the Bible is a collection of works written by various authors over several centuries. Think of the Bible as a diverse anthology of godly communication. It contains historical accounts, poetry, songs, letters of instruction and encouragement, messages from God sent through his representatives, and prophecies.

Most versions of the Bible have sixty-six books grouped into two sections: The Old Testament and the New Testament. The Old Testament contains thirty-nine books that precede and anticipate Jesus. The New Testament includes twenty-seven books and covers Jesus's life and the work of his followers.

The reference notations in the Bible, such as Romans 3:23, are analogous to line numbers in a Shakespearean play. They serve as a study aid. Since the Bible is much longer and more complex than a play, its reference notations are more involved.

As already mentioned, the Bible is an amalgam of books, or sections, such as Genesis, Matthew, or Acts. These are the names given to them, over time, based on the piece's author, audience, or purpose.

In the 1200s, each book was divided into chapters, such as Acts 2 or Psalm 23. In the 1500s, the chapters were further subdivided into verses, such as John 3:16. Let's use this as an example.

The name of the book (John) appears first, followed by the chapter number (3), a colon, and then the verse number (16). Sometimes called a chapter-verse reference notation, this helps people quickly find a specific text regardless of their version of the Bible.

Although the goal was to place these chapter and verse divisions at logical breaks, they sometimes seem arbitrary. Therefore, it's good practice to read what precedes and follows each passage you're studying. The text before or after it may contain relevant insights into the portion you're exploring.

Here's how to look up a specific passage in the Bible based on its reference: Most Bibles contain a table of contents, which gives the page number for the beginning of each book. Start there. Locate the book you want to read, and turn to that page. Then flip forward to the chapter you want. Last, skim that chapter to locate the specific verse.

If you want to read online, enter the reference into BibleGateway.com or BibleHub.com. Also check out the YouVersion app.

Learn more about the greatest book ever written at ABibleADay.com, which provides a Bible blog, summaries of the books of the Bible, a dictionary of Bible terms, Bible reading plans, and other resources.

ABOUT PETER DEHAAN

Peter DeHaan, PhD, wants to change the world one word at a time. His books and blog posts discuss God, the Bible, and church, geared toward spiritual seekers and church dropouts. Many people feel church has let them down, and Peter seeks to encourage them as they search for a place to belong.

But he's not afraid to ask tough questions or make religious people squirm. He's not trying to be provocative. Instead, he seeks truth, even if it makes people uncomfortable. Peter urges Christians to push past the status quo and reexamine how they practice their faith in every part of their lives.

Peter earned his doctorate, awarded with high distinction, from Trinity College of the Bible and Theological Seminary. He lives with his wife in beautiful Southwest Michigan and wrangles cross-word puzzles in his spare time.

A lifelong student of Scripture, Peter wrote the 1,000-page website ABibleADay.com to encourage people to explore the Bible, the greatest book ever written. His popular blog addresses biblical Christianity to build a faith that matters.

Read his blog, receive his newsletter, and learn more at PeterDeHaan.com.

BOOKS BY PETER DEHAAN

40-Day Bible Study Series

Dear Theophilus (the Gospel of Luke, formerly That You May Know)

Acts Bible Study (formerly Tongues of Fire)

Isaiah Bible Study (formerly For Unto Us)

Minor Prophets Bible Study (formerly Return to Me)

Job Bible Study (formerly I Hope in Him)

Living Water (John)

Love Is Patient (1 and 2 Corinthians)

Revelation Bible Study

1, 2, & 3 John Bible Study (formerly Love One Another)

Hebrews Bible Study

James and Jude Bible Study

Matthew Bible Study

1 & 2 Peter Bible Study

Mark Bible Study

Holiday Celebration Devotionals

The Advent of Jesus

The Passion of Jesus (Lent)

The Victory of Jesus (Easter)

The Ministry of Jesus

Thanksgiving with Jesus

New Year with Jesus

Bible Character Sketches Series

Women of the Bible

The Friends and Foes of Jesus

Old Testament Sinners and Saints

More Old Testament Sinners and Saints

Heroes and Heavies of the Apocrypha

200 Old Testament Sinners and Saints

Visiting Churches Series

52 Churches

The 52 Churches Workbook

More Than 52 Churches

The More Than 52 Churches Workbook

Visiting Online Church

Shopping for Church

Other Books

Elephant God

Jesus's Broken Church

Martin Luther's 95 Theses (formerly *95 Tweets*)

The Christian Church's LGBTQ Failure

Bridging the Sacred-Secular Divide (formerly *Woodpecker Wars*)

Beyond Psalm 150

How Big Is Your Tent?

For the latest list of all Peter's books, go to PeterDeHaan.com/books.